Elders Rising

Elders Rising

The Promise and Peril of Aging

Roland D. Martinson

Fortress Press
Minneapolis

ELDERS RISING
The Promise and Peril of Aging

Cover image: © istock 2018/mattjeacock/White Staircase
Cover design: Alisha Lofgren

Print ISBN: 978-1-5064-4054-5
eBook ISBN: 978-1-5064-4055-2

The paper used in this publication meets the minimum requirements of American National Standard for Information Sciences — Permanence of Paper for Printed Library Materials, ANSI Z329.48-1984.

Manufactured in the U.S.A.

CONTENTS

INTRODUCTION

This investigation of aging began with my own experience. At age seventy-five, I sensed changes in body, mind, and spirit. My joints often ached. I was stiff and moved more slowly. My skin was thinner and sagged. I looked different. Sometimes things I had known since childhood weren't "ready to mind." It took longer to read and digest the newspaper. Even though I moved more slowly, I had discretionary time to invest wherever and whenever. I had opportunities to do research or volunteer or play or just be; there were decisions to make about who to be and what to do.

All the while, I had more time for myself, more time to read and reflect. I spent more time with my classic cars and gardening. I biked and walked. I had time to play. My wife and I traveled. Relationships with my family and friends deepened. Big-picture considerations shifted. Faith perspectives and priorities became more important. My horizons and rhythms were different and changing. I referenced the past more than the future. Sometimes I wondered about when my life would end.

The Power of Conversation

As I talked with others about their aging experience and mine, we discovered common ground and spoke of acquaintances who were on their own pathways of aging. In these visits, I experienced the generative power of conversation and storytelling. I found wisdom in the stories and strength in the speaking and listening. What began as personal reflection on my aging became shared exploration of a complex and expansive season of life.

The conversations with others my age gave birth to a larger investigation. I wondered: might I speak with more people who are navigating the challenges of older adulthood? Might I listen, reflect on their stories, and learn from them as they make their way into what many gerontologists are calling a new era of aging? From these conversations and questions, a more extensive investigation of the everyday wisdom of people living life's third chapter was born.

Listening to Elders across the United States

In my investigation, I interviewed fifty-three people, ages sixty-two to ninety-seven. These diverse older adults come from all walks of life and live in six regions of the United States. I am grateful for their willingness to speak of their experiences. This foray into a new era of aging is dedicated to them, for their lives and stories are the heart and spirit of this effort to understand older adulthood more fully. While this group of older adults is representative of much of America, it is by no means a scientific sample; in fact, there is a particular bias among the elders I chose to interview. Because I was curious about the role of faith in the lives of older adults, the majority of the interviewees were identified through Christian faith communities. So, these elders are more into faith and faith communities than one might find in a cross section of older American adults. This sample of older adults is also skewed socioeconomically and racially; while four of the interviewees are living in the lowest of economic circumstances, and several others struggle to make ends meet, most of these elders are middle class. Forty-six of the interviewees are European American; four are African American; and three are Hispanic.

Many of my discoveries appear as individual stories. While all these stories and people are real, in order to provide confidentiality, the names of the persons and places in the stories are fictitious. Much from the interviews coalesced and illuminated themes that give shape and substance to this writing. Because I wanted those interviewed to speak in their own voices, they are often quoted to illustrate the themes that emerged.

Raising Provocative Questions

Along the way, interviewees raised provocative questions. To facilitate conversation and to encourage readers to reflect on their own experience, some of those questions are cited at the end of the chapters. And, because each chapter raises interesting issues for further reflection, suggestions for personal exploration and discussion appear at the end of chapters 1 through 15. Some interviewees and I imagine the possibilities of neighborhood organizations such as senior-citizen groups or congregations becoming Centers for Vital and Resilient Aging. To address this possibility, the last chapters of the book include suggestions for developing older-adult resources in local congregations and community organizations.

A Word about Possible Uses of This Book

This book begins with an investigation of aging in the United States and then moves on to biblical and theological understandings of elders and their role(s) in the church and society in chapter 2. In chapter 3, I draw from the stories of the fifty-three interviewees and from studies of aging in the current American context, viewed through the theological lenses of Scripture and Christian tradition.

I propose elderhood as a new life stage. The character of this new life stage is presented in chapters 4 through 10. Chapters 11 through 12 describe common older-adult challenges that require knowledge and skill if they are to be addressed constructively. Chapters 13 and 14 glean the investigation's most important discoveries and propose generative resources to be used by individual elders, families, congregations, and communities to enhance the quality of life for older adults and society.

This book has been written with conversation in mind. Each chapter concludes with discussion questions and exercises intended to encourage interaction. I encourage you to consider reading the book as a group and gathering to discuss its proposals, as well as to reflect on your own experience of aging.

I also imagine a group of older adults or a ministry staff of a church reading the book and gathering to explore the implications for enriching senior ministry. These conversations could lead to playful experiments, to an expansion of a congregation's service-oriented activities, or maybe even to launching bold new initiatives in the community.

Welcome to this conversation about elders rising!

1

The Age Wave and Early Navigators

Increasing longevity, declining fertility, and aging baby boomers are triggering an enormous age wave.

—Ken Dychtwald[1]

Who are the emerging role models of the new aging?

—Ken Dychtwald[2]

We are living an *age wave*. The huge, aging boomer generation is greatly increasing the population of older adults; there are sixty-five hundred more persons over the age of sixty-five in America every day. Elders are living longer and more robustly; if an older adult reaches sixty-five, they have an 87 percent chance of living to eighty-five. Geriatrics produces medicines and medical procedures that combat aging's chronic illnesses; older adults are healthier. Because they are healthier longer and disabled later and for fewer years, elder morbidity has been compressed. Gerontologists are developing services that enrich elders' lives. Sexologists are reporting increased sexual activity among seniors, and at older ages. Elders play more, travel more, exercise more. Many say seventy is the new fifty. More and more elders live well into their nineties.

The basic structures of security and channels of resources for elders are shifting. Politicians are debating the costs of public policies and services that provide financial support and health care for older adults—think viability of social security and medical insurance. Economists are addressing aging's financial challenges—witness the emergence of reverse mortgages. The unknowns and volume of cognitive impairment are mystifying and overwhelming the nation's capacity to give care—reference the increase in Alzheimer's disease and its attendant costs.

Senior-housing construction is booming; older adults are on waiting lists to get into *communities of care*. Extensive, specialized home-care services are now available almost everywhere. Scientific journals, novels, newspapers, magazines, television programs, movies, videos, blogs, businesses, advertisers, and more investigate aging and offer an expanding array of counsel and products for seniors. All this provides evidence of senior citizens more broadly and deeply present and engaged in the fabric of our culture.[3]

This "changing face of aging" is among the most powerful forces shaping our society. In fact, the new realities of aging and the speed of change generated by the age wave are outpacing the capacity of scientists and leaders to investigate and adapt to the disruptions. Neurologists are playing catch-up in their research on Alzheimer's disease, politicians struggle to come to terms with underfunded entitlements, and assisted-living communities can't find enough skilled staff. So older adults are forging their own ways of coping and thriving as they live the uncharted territory of aging in a hugely different era than that of their parents or grandparents.

This investigation listened to the stories of these everyday pioneers in this new era of aging and gleaned their wisdom. As I spoke with older adults across the country, I met early navigators who are effectively riding the early twenty-first-century age wave. The fifty-three men and women I interviewed provide a picture of the challenging and complex worlds of older adults as well as their courageous, imaginative responses to these new realities. Six interviewees and their stories provide an introduction to that courage and imagination I discovered from these early navigators.

Meet . . .

> This "changing face of aging" is among the most powerful forces shaping our society.

- Bill, age sixty-eight, resilient and vital in the face of loss;
- Virginia, age seventy-one, anchored yet unfinished and searching;
- Jake, age seventy-five, "spark plug" volunteer extraordinaire;

- Sherry, age eighty-one, curious bridge builder;
- Burt, age ninety-two, grieving, resilient storyteller; and
- Dale, age ninety-seven, persistent, adaptive humorist.

These trailblazers provide glimpses of the promise and peril inherent in the pace, in the breadth and depth, of the challenges and opportunities for older adults in the twenty-first-century age wave.

Bill: Resilient and Vital Amid Loss

Bill is sixty-eight; early retirement from his "envisioned lifelong career" began abruptly eighteen years ago when his wife died of ovarian cancer, leaving him to parent two sons, ages twelve and nineteen. Because his career as a highly mobile troubleshooter for a large pharmaceutical company was incompatible with his new role as primary caregiver, Bill left his powerful position to devote his time to fatherhood.

His wife's death, the loss of his career, and his new parental responsibilities overwhelmed Bill. He reflects, "The loss of my wife and the simultaneous loss of a challenging career disrupted my identity and purpose for living." Navigating his sons' adolescence as a single parent was unfamiliar, complicated, and confusing. Confused and overwhelmed, Bill became isolated, gained weight, and went into a physical, emotional, social, and spiritual tailspin.

Bill's malaise and downward spiral were interrupted by inspirational ideas in a book he was reading and a generative question put to him in a conversation. Bill remembers, "Reading

Bob Buford's *Halftime: Moving from Success to Significance* opened my mind and spirit to different life possibilities and metrics, placed my feet on solid ground, and provided me a horizon of new possibilities and purpose." About the same time, theologian and church historian Martin Marty posed a question to Bill: What is your wife's legacy? Buford's book and Marty's question became a bridge from the peril of Bill's malaise to a pathway of promise. Bill says of crossing this bridge: "A season of disruption and the dark night of the spirit were transformed into the beginnings of a new life lived for the sake of others."

Shortly after "rising from his malaise," Bill met a single mother and remarried. This second marriage is a gift and hugely engrossing as Bill and his "new" wife of fourteen years "work at building and maintaining" their relationship with each other and their relationships with their own and each other's sons. Bill says, "Each day brings significant challenges as we work out complexities of a second marriage, differing parenting expectations, multiple sibling relationships, and integrating a blended family."

Upon leaving his employment, Bill received a large separation package from the organization where he had spent his career. He combined that money with his experience as a corporate problem solver and his knowledge and skill as an organizational system developer into a new calling. Bill says, "I reinvented myself as an organizational consultant and venture capitalist who coaches leaders in the nonprofit sector to better manage personnel and steward funds." Bill's unique niche enterprise contributes greatly to civic organizations' capacities to more effectively and sustainably serve their communities.

Loss continues to shape Bill's life. Over the last two decades, he has lost his first wife, his career, his parents, his grandfather, and his mother-in-law, and he has witnessed his sons' disengagement from their communities of faith. Directly tending the ongoing presence and pain of his losses steadies Bill's emotions and strengthens his spirit. Bill reflects: "These losses and healing have informed my appreciation for what I have, and what I can do to serve others." Resiliency in the face of his losses is one of the taproots of Bill's energetic, multidimensional, purposeful life.

As he reflects on these experiences, Bill says, "I am discovering a 'formula for vitality,' a way of life born of difficulty, grounded in faith and hope, and expressed through mindfulness, purpose, and vision."

At sixty-eight, Bill's vitality stems from his constructive attention to his many losses, his imaginative adaptation to major life disruptions beyond his control, and his effective utilization of his skills and passions to serve others. Bill is a resilient, generative early elder.

Virginia: Anchored but Restless and Unfinished

Virginia is seventy-one and unsettled. She feels she has accomplished little of significance in her life. She voices her regret: "I should have made more of myself."

Virginia retired at sixty-nine, earlier than she intended due to pressures at work; she was a supervisor in an understaffed department working under unreasonable production expectations. She soon discovered that she could not afford to live on her social security and pension without depleting her savings. Frustrated and needing to supplement her income, she went back to retail work part-time. When offered a full-time position "out on the floor, always on [her] feet," she declined knowing that it would be "too much for me."

Presently, Virginia works part-time for a nonprofit organization coordinating programs on sexual health and abuse prevention. Virginia says, "The mission of the organization and the people with whom I work are a good fit for me; I look forward to getting more hours of work, and, with additional hours, a larger salary."

Although married three times, Virginia is currently single. She has a son from her second marriage who lives across the country and is married with one child. There is great geographical and emotional distance between Virginia and her son and his family. She laments, "We are not close; in fact, our relationship is significantly conflicted."

For the last seven months, Virginia has been dating a man ten years younger than she, a pattern that she recognizes was present in her previous relationships. Virginia reflects, "I enjoy the companionship of our dating, but I do not see our relationship heading for marriage."

Virginia is artistic and a skilled interior designer. She has just redesigned and remodeled her condo. Even though she greatly enjoys interior design and has demonstrated significant capabilities as a home-redevelopment consultant, Virginia downplays her talent and is reticent to accept the affirmation of those who delight in her artistry.

Her faith community is the spiritual and social center of Virginia's life. Virginia reports, "At church I'm accepted for who I am. I make friends there; what's more, the community provides me stability and a setting in which to express my artistic side." Given the hurt and scars that Virginia carries from her past relationships and life disappointments, her church, she says, is a "welcome place of forgiveness, hospitality, and healing."

While Virginia's restlessness continues, she is embedded in a community that authentically and constructively accompanies her as she works out the structure and meaning of the financial, social, and spiritual dimensions of her life.

At seventy-one, Virginia is anchored yet at sea; a restless early elder.

Jake: Spark Plug Volunteer Extraordinaire

Jake is seventy-five and rejoices to be "enjoying a fresh and productive season of my life." For the last five years, Jake has volunteered at a community life center that serves low-income seniors. He waits tables, leads singing, supports staff, and "does whatever needs to be done." Recently, upon the nomination of those he serves and supported by the staff with whom he volunteers, Jake was named Volunteer of the Year by area civic leaders. It is easy to see why; simply walking along with Jake among the persons and communities he serves is to be immersed in an aura of compassion, dignity, and hope.

During much of his adult life, Jake owned a real-estate company that served low-income home buyers. He says, "My business and its mission of providing low-cost housing was my calling." During the recent recession, Jake lost his company and with it his income and his "life's purpose." During this period of disintegration, his marriage fell apart. In response to the loss of his company, Jake went back to school and reeducated himself. His age, however, makes finding work difficult, and Jake hasn't landed a job.

With the loss of his business, and without a job, Jake was without income. He was left to live on his social security, which makes for an austere lifestyle. So, Jake lives in a small efficiency apartment in senior housing and relies on his bike and public transportation to get around. Battered by this huge disruption in his life, Jake's primary relationships significantly diminished. He tersely sums it up: "I was devastated."

Now Jake excitedly exclaims, "My discovery of the senior-center community and the opportunity to volunteer saved my life." At the senior center, he rediscovered himself and found a new calling that he describes as being "claimed by a caring community" that needed him and his gifts. Jake is a gifted musician who was introduced to music in the seventh grade and has participated in music ever since. Now, he leads his peers at the senior center in making music for each other and for the community.

Jake's outgoing personality and genuine interest and delight in other people are contagious. As he moves through the senior-center community, meeting each person on their own terms, he ignites excitement and hope that fills the room. Jake sees himself as a "spark plug," a role model for older people, especially older people of color. Jake says: "My primary passion is to encourage people of color to become and stay healthy. I challenge those who have bad habits and poor nutrition to alter their lifestyles and eat differently. I encourage them to be active and exercise, to work out as I do at the local YMCA attached to the senior center where I volunteer." Jake seeks out black elders—especially those living in public housing—listens to their stories, and discerns with them their needs, strengths, and interests. He invites them via the senior center to live into a "redis-covered season of life."

> My primary passion is to encourage people of color to become and stay healthy.

Jake's early life was difficult. "I was delivered at home; by the grace of God I came through," Jake says with gratitude. His first marriage ended in divorce because he and his wife couldn't have children, and she didn't want to adopt. During his second marriage, he and his wife adopted a son, who now has two children and lives some distance from Jake. So, Jake says appreciatively, "The senior center and my church are my 'extended family of focus.'" The church that Jake attends is a multiracial congregation with a rich ethnic mix that he values highly. This faith community is a receptive environment for Jake to exercise his musical talents, to be a valued elder, and to receive the love, affirmation, and message that feeds his spirit.

Jake's church and his volunteer work at the senior community center are the heart and structure of his vital life, lived in the face of financial austerity. He claims "nothing is more valuable than being able to give back . . . especially among your peers."

Jake is an adaptive, passionate, inspirational middle elder.

Sherry: Bridge Builder

"Timing and location are everything," Sherry asserts as she describes the latest period of her life. At eighty-one, Sherry recalls the disruption when, at sixty-eight, she retired and returned to the United States after eight years of living and working in Africa. She remembers "big questions arising from the disruption that came with my retirement." There were questions like "Who am I? Who am I without my old roles, without my work? Who am I in this new time, this new place? Is retirement like being on a 'forever vacation'? Am I now more of a parent? More of a grandparent? Or am I of no value? Am I finished?"

With the disruption and big questions swirling around her, Sherry's transition from one continent to another, and her movement away from public roles, began in the United States near where her daughter and son live. There, as an early step in her reorientation, she more fully engaged in her family's life.

Soon there was more. Sherry became a consultant to her national church regarding their ministry in Tanzania. Because of her commitment to diversity and its impact on professors and courses, Sherry was also drafted to guide the reconstruction of a global seminar at the college where she had taught before going to Africa. Sherry currently teaches a course at an area college one semester a year.

Sherry loves to write and read. She emphatically points out, "I decided to write during retirement; it's a way for this introvert to be creative; words have become my companions."

Sherry began by writing her mother's biography. Then came a book on education. Next she wrote about dealing with dying because of the sudden deaths of her husband at age forty-five and both her parents. Sherry is working with an African author on a new book.

Sherry is a voracious reader: "Reading feeds my writing." And writing feeds Sherry. In her book on dying, she discusses her family history, where death is an earlier than average experience that her family members and others don't talk about. Sherry observes, "Society has little experience talking about death . . . especially the slow incapacitation of people, most especially older adults."

People and relationships are the heart of Sherry's life. Her son and daughter both live nearby; she is pleased that her grandson, Stephen, is in a national service corps. After family, the next most-important piece of Sherry's life is church, especially her present congregation.

Sherry's congregation is an interracial, intercultural, intergenerational mix that deepens and broadens her consciousness. She's lived in multicultural communities around the world and savors the richness of difference that is everywhere present in her faith community. Speaking of her role in her congregation, she says, "I sit at the back of the church and get into conversations with young people. I like not being responsible, but accompanying, being in conversation. I don't lobby, I work to bring people together . . . to listen . . . to speak and agree to disagree if necessary. I seek to broaden their bandwidth; to learn to live the questions. So I listen to the young . . . especially those who are different."

Sherry's big questions and her struggles and challenges are ongoing. She wonders, "How do I be social as a single, widowed, older woman?" She muses, "I'm seeking to redefine 'aloneness' as a friend, as a gift as well as depravation and loss." A balanced schedule of activities and group experiences are important to Sherry. She says, "I like one-on-one substantive conversations better than being in a large group; I have less capacity to track a room with lots of stuff going on."

> I seek to broaden their bandwidth; to learn to live the questions.

Wellness is paramount in Sherry's life. She has worn a back brace since high school, so she is careful about bending or lifting. She exercises regularly; she especially appreciates walking outside, listening to and seeing nature, so she walks around lakes. Mindfulness is also important to Sherry. She values "intentional mind, spirit, and body awareness and integration." She says "Candles, meditation, and books are my friends; NPR is my friend . . . especially its music." Sherry is most attentive in the morning, so she writes then.

As Sherry has lived the big questions, her reflections on her life and life's big picture have yielded strong convictions. Sherry asserts, "Life is an extraordinary gift. I'm deeply grateful for my life." And "Words matter. Writing and speaking give people handles on life."

Sherry is a thoughtful and centered middle elder.

Burt: Grieving Storyteller

Burt is ninety-two. His life, full of years and experience, affords him rich and expansive material for writing and videography. Before his wife died, Burt wrote and compiled a scripted photographic book of her life. In the years since her death, he has written stories about her, their relationship, and his grieving. His expansive chronicling of the eventful periods of his life continues as he produces videos on subjects ranging from World War II aircraft to the beauty of imaginative landscaping and magnificent flower gardens. Burt is leaving a legacy in story.

Burt asserts, "Leukemia, skin cancer, prostate cancer, and pneumonia have come and battered my life, but through the powers of modern medicine, my strong will, and my supportive communities, each illness has been overcome; at ninety-two, I'm in generally good health and deeply grateful." He goes on, "I am sharp mentally, but slower, meaning I have to work at concentration." It's still there; it just requires more work and takes longer.

Burt lives at Woolsey Homes, which he describes as a "well-designed community of care." After moving early in his retirement from his big house into a condominium, Woolsey's high-quality, well-executed, accessible design and strong interactive culture are currently a good fit for Burt. Such a good fit did not come by accident; Burt interviewed more than twenty-five senior resident homes before choosing Woolsey, and then was on a long waiting list to get in.

Burt's days and weeks are as full as he can comfortably manage. He has traveled extensively and continues to travel domestically and internationally. He was recently in Japan, participating as a World War II veteran in an Honor Flight. Elsie, his adopted daughter, who is his "essential traveling companion," made it possible for him to go. Burt still designs landscapes and plants flowers as a volunteer in his community. All this Burt "works into" his schedule of writing and videography.

Because of his longevity, Burt continues to endure many losses, including the loss of his wife of over sixty years. Burt reflects, "Tending my grief is always with me; it is a major concern and an ongoing task in my life. On the way, storytelling, verbally and visually, are my pathways of healing and bridge to the future."

Burt is grateful; he credits his rich life to "my intelligent mother and affirming aunt who encouraged and disciplined my boyhood curiosity, set me off on an interesting, active life that continues into my nineties." In the military during World War II, Burt became a radio operator and was introduced to the "big world" and the importance of faithfully shouldering responsibility for others. While in the service, he became a Christian, which Burt asserts "significantly shapes my values and anchors my relationships." After the war, he became a landscape

> Tending my grief is always with me; it is a major concern and an ongoing task in my life.

artist. During his career, Burt's intelligence, imagination, and diligence led him to work overseeing major building projects in one of America's largest cities.

Burt was given a good start, he built well on those foundations, and he is finishing strong. All is woven together in stories— stories providing wisdom for those around him now and stories providing wisdom for future generations.

Burt is a legacy-making, generation-bridging, restive late elder.

Dale: Adaptive Humorist

Dale is ninety-seven. His days are taken up with life's basic tasks of, as he puts it, "staying clean, getting dressed, eating and remembering where I put my clothes and dishes . . . and where I last left my books and 'writing tools.'" These tools are the staples of Dale's ongoing life of "the mind and spirit."

Dale says his biggest challenge is "keeping track of my life . . . day to day." He often forgets where he left things. He knows that he is extremely forgetful and adapts by labeling his basic "utensils and the places where they belong" as well as designing redundancy systems as backups for finding what he can't locate or remember. His adaptive "external memory system" mostly works, but when it doesn't, Dale gets angry with himself because of his cognitive impairment; he wryly speaks of these "momentary fits" as his "temper with himself."

Retired thirty-five years from his career as an office machine repairman, Dale sees his "latest period of life set off by the move from my home to a senior assisted-living facility." The move was frustratingly disruptive, a period of time during which Dale says, "I lost my mind and lost my bearings." Prior to the move, Dale had mapped his house and developed the redundant location and reminder systems that structured his life and thereby provided safety, comfort, and time to read and write. After thirteen months in his new assisted-living residence, Dale says: "I have finally gotten my smaller living space mapped and all that I need day to day labeled so that I feel 'at home' and have my bearings and mind back."

Dale possess a wry, easygoing sense of humor. The lilt in his voice, the glint in his eye, and his ready smile combine with his rich vocabulary and imaginative life adaptions to generate an impressive, authentic, and hopeful presence. Dale is at the same time fragile, resilient, and funny; he is simultaneously hugely present and forgetful.

As an introvert who loves to read and write, especially parodies and other forms of humor, Dale says, "I don't need, in fact don't like, having large groups of people around me. I enjoy time alone writing humorous stories. Currently, however, I'm afraid I watch too much television."

While graced with humor and hope, Dale is no stranger to pain and suffering. He married late, a marriage wherein he says he "endured twenty-one years of misery" with an addicted spouse; they eventually divorced. The memories are still painful.

Dale had a "dysfunctional upbringing" in which he was provided life's physical necessities but had little companionship and was given no sense of being loved and affirmed. Dale reports: "I have little memory of anyone, my parents or kids at school, ever playing with me. I know these experiences are part of my clumsiness in relationships and my extreme introversion." In this "arid relational background," Dale's adopted daughter stands out as a "shining jewel" who accompanies him in working out his life. Dale gratefully says, "my daughter and my grandson and my faith community who accept me as I am and drive me around and enjoy my stories are enough of the right people I need in my life."

Dale is healthy yet physically fragile. He walks slightly bent over; he has a walker and cane that he never uses, yet he gets around just fine, albeit slowly. Dale is often alone but rarely lonely; he has the right people when he needs them. Dale quit driving at age ninety-six; now he has people drive him to his appointments. They listen to his stories when they are a captive audience in the car together.

Dale is significantly incapacitated yet multiply-able. At ninety-seven, Dale is a wonderfully funny, imaginatively adaptive, ingenious late elder.

Navigating the Age Wave

These fascinating elders are making their way through the age wave's thirty-year stage of older adulthood. On the way, they are encountering challenging disruptions that come with aging:

- Significant losses
- Unsettling forces beyond their control

- Interrupted life plans
- Crushed dreams
- Multifaceted physical decline
- Cognitive impairment
- Multiple chronic diseases and illnesses
- Isolation and alienation
- Insufficient incomes
- Multiple relocations

These elders are most certainly vulnerable. Yet, even as they are vulnerable, they are resilient and vital. They exhibit courage and imagination in the face of challenging circumstances. Each one of these six elders has, in their own way, honestly engaged and grieved major losses and moved on with their lives. Bill has redesigned his family relationships and work in response to his wife's death, the need to parent his two boys, and the call to a new career. Virginia has gone back to work because she was unable to live on her social security and savings. At ninety-two, Burt has outlived most of his friends and his wife of sixty years. Though his grief is always with him, Burt has, through his writing and videography, forged new ways to heal and reorient himself. Like Bill, Virginia, and Burt, the elders interviewed have reconstructed the

> They exhibit courage and imagination in the face of challenging circumstances.

frameworks and pathways of their worlds multiple times. These elders are enduring and managing the perils of aging. This exploration of their stories aims to pass their strength and wisdom on to others.

There is also great promise in their stories. Each elder has surrounded himself or herself with relationships and, in many cases, faith communities in which they are cared for and in which they care for others. They participate in groups where they experience life-giving relationships and make a difference. Jake finds a home in the adult care center and congregation where he inspires and guides older adults as they reenvision their lives. So too for Sherry, who is immersed in a multiracial, multicultural congregation where she feels at home while she guides young people as they pursue their life questions in mutually enriching relationships. These early navigators are adapting and compensating for aging's increasing limitations, even as they are forging quality lives in complex contexts and challenging circumstances.

Each of these early navigators has discovered and is harnessing their passions and gifts to make contributions to the larger common good. Jake's positive personality, musical talents, and delight in other people fill him and others with meaning and joy. Sherry is writing books, consulting with churches and universities, and teaching college classes. Dale, at ninety-seven, is writing parodies and amusing those who drive him to his appointments. As a group, these elders are productive, hopeful, and enjoying life. They embody the unique richness of the promise of what has become a thirty-year period of older adulthood. They are ordinary elders navigating the twenty-first-century age wave. They are elders rising.

Exploration and Discussion

1. Ken Dychtwald writes: "Increased longevity, declining fertility and aging Baby Boomers are triggering an enormous *age wave*." What evidence of the age wave do you experience in your life? What is its impact on you? What is its impact on your family?

2. Who are society's emerging models of aging? What are they like?

3. Upon retirement and relocation, one of the elders described in the chapter asked: "Who am I? Who am I without my old roles, without my work? Who am I in this new time, this new place? Is retirement like being on a 'forever vacation'?" How would you answer her questions in reference to yourself?

4. Look again at the list of challenging disruptions elders are encountering (p. 24–25). How many of these disruptions have you encountered? What has been their impact on you?

5. One of the elders said of the disruptions in his life: "A season of disruption and the dark night of the spirit were transformed into the beginnings of a new life lived for the sake of others." What makes such a transformation possible? How have you responded to the disruptions that have come with your aging?

2

Aging and the Christian Faith

I am embedded in faith and it's embedded in me; it's in my bones, in my being; I regularly ask God: "Lord, what do you want me to do today?"

—Sarah, age seventy-eight

Love is God's way of giving life; love is God's way of being in charge; love is the big thing; love never ends; love is the lens though which I look at life.

—Betsy, age seventy-nine

Spirituality is less about getting it right; it's more about the community of the church, about Jesus as a source of strength, as a forever presence around us that becomes mostly thanksgiving and doing together.

—Sally, age eighty-four

As the elders interviewed were navigating a new era of aging, faith and faith communities emerged as major factors in their lives. Nearly all of the fifty-three interviewees referenced the Christian faith as they spoke of their values, relationships, and activities. Most of the interviewees spoke directly about their faith and their congregations as contributors to their decision-making, well-being, and hope for the future. At age ninety-two, Burt credited his faith community's support as a major factor in his will to live as he battled leukemia, skin cancer, prostate cancer, and pneumonia. Like Burt, many of the elders spoke of their congregations as "spiritual and social oases."

The elders interviewed represent what gerontologists have discovered about religion and older adults. Their studies reveal that seniors significantly influence and, in turn, are profoundly shaped by American religion. Approximately 42 percent of church members in the United States are sixty-five and older. More seniors attend worship than any other age group. They make up huge numbers of congregational volunteers. They give a significant portion of their churches' offerings. In a 2009 Pew Study, 66 percent of persons sixty-five and older indicated that religion was important to them and 34 percent indicated that their faith and its practice had grown in importance during their older

> For seniors, faith is a prime factor in their identity, and their faith practices are sources of meaning and hope.

adulthood.[1] For seniors, faith is a prime factor in their identity, and their faith practices are sources of meaning and hope. Their faith communities are networks of sustained, trustworthy relationships. Spirituality and religion are important to a large majority of seniors who are deeply bonded to lives of faith in mutually beneficial exchanges of presence and action. The elders in this study were no exception.

So, what aspects of the Christian faith and their faith communities are impacting these elders? More importantly, how might these factors of faith constructively inform individual elders and elderhood?

Elders and Communities of Faith

Most of the fifty-three interviewees spoke of their church as a safe and supportive community. For some, their faith communities were their primary relationships, providing the family they don't have. This is Tony's experience at age seventy-two. Tony was sent away from home by his father when he was eight. He slept on the streets and made a living working in the fields, panhandling, and dealing drugs. Tony was married and divorced early; one of his ex-wives is a heroin addict. Tony has been cut off from his family, and almost no one comes to visit him at the low-cost care facility that is his home. Tony's most important relationship is with the person from church who faithfully comes to visit him, brings him malted milks, and takes him to baseball games. Tony speaks of the visitor from the church as his best friend. Now, at his advanced age, Tony has a close friend for the first time in his life—someone he can trust, someone he can count on, and someone who respects and takes delight in him.

The church also provides primary relationships for Dale at age ninety-seven. Dale sees his congregation as his "accompanying community," the people who drive him to shop and to his appointments while listening to his whimsical, humorous writing. Dale says of his congregation and his adopted daughter: "These are all the people I need in my life. They are not many, but they are essential, and they are enough."

For most of the interviewees, their faith communities do not provide their closest, primary relationships but rather generate important secondary relationships—the friendships, the support, and the places of belonging that anchor and enrich their lives. Betty and her husband, Dan, view their faith community as the "prime force," the "focusing community" that provides their "social base." Betty says, "Our congregation combines our most significant friendships with a sense of purpose through the mission work we do together; our faith community is the social and spiritual center of our lives." Similarly, Betsy and her husband attended a Bible study together with four other couples for twenty-five years. This group of couples became their social and spiritual home. Now with her husband gone, Betsy identifies "these spiritual and social companions as a mainstay of my life."

For nearly all of the interviewees, faith communities functioned in some way as a combination of spiritual oasis and social wellspring.

Elders in the Christian Tradition

In addition to faith communities providing trusted relationships and generative places of belonging, the narrative of the Christian faith informed and shaped the interviewees' views of themselves and their place in the world. Their beliefs in God's presence and action provided the frameworks for their lives, sustained them in crises, and anchored their hopes for the future. Some of their faith tenets were explicit, but most of their convictions regarding their current season of life lay beneath the surface of their activities, in their beliefs and values. Their lives were consciously and unconsciously, explicitly and implicitly informed by the Christian God story as recorded in Scripture and reflected in their Christian traditions.

Elders and Scripture

Much of Scripture's view of humans and the human situation was reflected in the stories of the interviewees. In the Old Testament, humans bear *imago Dei*, the image of God, meaning humans are created by God in God's image, enlivened by God's breath, blessed, and given the responsibility of co-managing the creation. Humans have their identity, their value, their place in the scheme of things not on the basis of their age or their looks or their abilities. Rather, human identity and value are established by the action of the designer of the universe who posits dignity in every person. As Betsy, one of the elders says, "Love is God's way of giving life." Human dignity is not earned, and neither is it generated by status, attractiveness, or age; it is given by

God's loving, creative action. Elders are included. And most of these elders know it "in their bones."

Teaching and Modeling the God Story

This human dignity and wholeness afforded elders in the Old Testament takes shape and is given expression in Israel, with its Mid-eastern desert culture, during the agricultural age. In Israel, elders were to be honored and cared for, in part because they played a major role in the family's preparation of the next generation for faith and life. Thus, one of the Ten Commandments stipulates: "Honor your father and your mother, so that your days may be long upon the land that the Lord your God is giving you" (Exod 20:12). This is the first commandment with a promise

> Human dignity is not earned, and neither is it generated by status, attractiveness, or age; it is given by God's loving, creative action.

Elder parents and grandparents, and with them all elders, are to be respected and honored in part because they assist in preparing the next generations for society's spiritual and ethical responsibilities. While elders may not be able to do all the hard work of providing food, shelter, and clothing, they are valued because they are able and expected to pass on the stories of faith and life, stories that establish the identity and values of their children, their children's children, and ultimately the tribe and nation. Moreover, they are to be role models and mentors of faith, values, and behavior. These roles are expressed in Moses's words in Deuteronomy 6:1–9 (emphasis added):

> Now this is the commandment—the statues and the ordinances—that the Lord your God charged me to teach you to observe in the land that you are about to cross into and occupy, so that *you and your children and your children's children may fear the Lord your God all the days of your life*, and keep all his decrees and his commandments that I am commanding you, *so that your days may be long*. Hear therefore, O Israel, and observe them diligently, so that it may go well with you, and so that you may multiply greatly in a land flowing with milk and honey, as the Lord, the God of your ancestors, has promised you.
>
> Hear, O Israel: The Lord is our God, the Lord alone. You shall love the Lord your God with all your heart, and with all your soul, and with all your might. Keep these words that I am commanding you today in your heart. *Recite them to your children* and talk about them when you are at home and when you are away, when you lie down and when you rise. Bind them as a sign on your hand, fix them as an emblem on your forehead, and write them on the doorposts of your house and on your gates.

In the Old Testament, *old age* and *fullness of years* were understood as affording the experience, knowledge, skill, and time to teach and model the God story, which included the faith- and life-enhancing narratives, values, and ways of life. Elders were to pass on their faith and life experiences, their broad exposure to life's mystery and messiness, and their lifelong inter-action with God through prayer and study, all of which uniquely qualified them for their roles as teachers and mentors.

One of the elders interviewed provides this kind of faith-and-values mentoring among her family and at her church. Earlier (p. 17), we introduced Sherry, age eighty-one, who has written her mother's biography, making her mother's story of principled integrity and active faith available to her children and grand-children. Sherry has also written about the sudden deaths of her mother, father, and husband in order to, as she puts it, "generate a more open conversation about death and dying from the per-spective of the faith tradition's realistic hope." Sherry expands her mentoring activities by getting into conversations with the young people at her church about faith's questions—most espe-cially about the faith questions these young people are asking.

Elders Essential and Valued

Throughout the Old Testament, there are statements and stories regarding the peculiar responsibilities and capacities of the aged for these essential societal roles.

> Remember the days of old;
>> consider the years long past;
> ask your father, and he will inform you;
>> your elders, and they will tell you.
> (Deut 32:7)

The righteous flourish like the palm tree,
    and grow like a cedar in Lebanon.
They are planted in the house of the Lord;
    they flourish in the courts of our God.
In old age they still produce fruit;
    they are always green and full of sap,
showing that the Lord is upright.
(Ps 92:12–15)

So even to old age and gray hairs,
    O God, do not forsake me,
until I proclaim your might
    to all the generations to come.
(Ps 71:18)

The glory of youths is their strength,
    but the beauty of the aged is their gray hair.
(Prov 20:29)

You shall rise before the aged and defer to the old; and
you shall fear your God: I am the Lord. (Lev 19:32)

I said, "Let days speak,
    and many years teach wisdom."
(Job 32:7)

Is wisdom with the aged,
    and understanding in length of days?
(Job 12:12)

In their Old Testament roles as leaders, teachers, and mentors, elders often are said to have the capacity and qualification of *wisdom*. So, what is the wisdom that these elders in Scripture possess and are to transmit? An assortment of Old Testament characters and events lift up and flesh out wisdom as a significant component in individual, familial, and national well-being. Among these characters and events, older adults exemplifying wisdom stand out as they lead at critical moments in Israel's history.

Abraham and Sarah

When Abram was ninety-nine years old, the Lord appeared to Abram, and said to him, "I am God Almighty; walk before me, and be blameless. And I will make my covenant between me and you, and will make you exceedingly numerous. . . . I have made you the ancestor of a multitude of nations. I will make you exceedingly fruitful; and I will make nations of you. . . . And I will give to you, and to your offspring after you, the land where you are now an alien." (Gen 17:1–8)

While some of Abraham and Sarah's earlier life is described in Genesis, God's covenantal promise comes to Abraham at age ninety-nine and to Sarah, who is but ten years younger. The promise entails faithfulness to God's claim on their lives, giving birth to a son, owning a land in perpetuity, and becoming a blessing to all nations. Abraham and Sarah are given new names to signal their new identity and mission. The unfolding of God's establishment of a people through whom the world will be blessed begins with a barren couple well beyond child-bearing age.

The promise is audacious (conceiving a child at their age), and arbitrary forces challenge their very lives (family conflict and hostile nations). Even so, at their advanced ages, Abraham and Sarah show surprising resilience. They bear a son, face down their enemies, and prove trustworthy in the face of God's testing. With faithfulness, they struggle to assure God's covenant promises and claims. They wrestle with doubt and fear as they raise Isaac and Ishmael and launch the family that will bless all nations. Theirs is a messy world, and not every decision they make is perfect, but by faith Abraham and Sarah begin a mission they will not see the end of. They are examples of elders rising in trust and faithfulness to God as the foundation of wisdom.

Moses and Aaron

Moses and Aaron did . . . just as the Lord commanded them. Moses was eighty years old and Aaron was eighty-three when they spoke to Pharaoh. (Exod 7:6–7)

Moses and Aaron are already elders when they confront Pharaoh. They complain of the oppression of the Hebrew people and demand their freedom. They persevere and become the leaders of the Israelites' exodus from Egypt and their long journey through the wilderness to the promised land. During this wilderness journey, Moses wrestles with God as he chafes under his difficult leadership responsibilities, but he delivers God's Ten Commandments and leads God's people to the boundary of the land God promised to Abraham and Sarah and their descendants. Moses dies before the people cross over the Jordan River to settle in the land, but with God's guidance and empowerment, Moses gets Israel there. In his elder years, he rises as a courageous, faithful, and wise elder.

Mordecai

During Israel's exile in Persia, Mordecai mentors his adopted cousin Esther in a life-and-death situation. In spite of great risk to himself and to Esther, Mordecai's faithfulness and wisdom prove to be crucial to the survival of the Jewish people. Esther and Mordecai have a long, trusted relationship. Mordecai adopts Esther when she is young and raises her as though she is his own child. Eventually, both Mordecai and Esther move into positions of influence in the Persian court—Esther through her beauty and Mordecai via his wisdom and strategic sensibilities. Mordecai is Esther's parent, teacher, guide, support, and mentor, most especially as Esther confronts Persian king Ahasuerus on behalf of her people. Esther, with Mordecai at her side as wise counsel, saves the Israelites in exile from destruction.

> In his elder years, he rises as a courageous, faithful, and wise elder.

Job

When we look for an example of a biblical person who experienced seemingly senseless and excruciating loss and suffering, we think of Job. In the prime of life, he loses his children and his livestock. And he is afflicted with loathsome sores from head to toe. He faces the kinds of personal peril we all fear, especially as we reach our elder years. In spite of this personal calamity, Job reflects on his experience and listens to the counsel of those who advise him. As he wrestles with faith in the shadow of life's destructiveness and mystery, he recites God's decree as truth: "The fear of the Lord, that is wisdom; and to depart from evil is understanding" (Job 28:28). At the end of a full and prosperous life, Job not only wrestles with the destruction of his earthly possessions, relationships, and security but struggles with his understanding of and trust in God. Aging, ailing Job becomes an example to believers exploring vexing questions about a good, powerful God and human suffering. Job, a wise elder, provides an honest, realistic picture of struggling with and trusting in God's faithfulness in the face of destruction, despair, and doubt.

A Description of Elder Wisdom

Through the witness of Old Testament elders, there emerges in the Scriptures a rich portrait of wisdom—wisdom exercised by elders at critical junctures in the history of the people of God. In this portrait, the elders' fear (or honoring) of God is the beginning of their wisdom. This wisdom is grounded in recognition of God's power and holiness, in belief in God's authority, and in an ongoing, though struggling, response to God's gracious love.

Centered and framed in a firsthand relationship with God, their wisdom is formed by studying the law and the prophets and faithfully working the law and the prophet's living traditions. Their wisdom is knowing and enacting moral behavior. Their wisdom is humbly, courageously doing the right thing even in the face of opposition, rejection, and danger.

These biblical elders have perspective. Their wisdom is seen in their interpretation of present events, ideas, and actions in the light of the big picture and long view of God's purposes. Their wisdom is critical reflection on and learning from the past, especially from their mistakes, and investing these learnings in the enhancement of God's people's present and future.

> This biblical wisdom is embodied in humble, substantive elders who are imperfect and limited and yet trust God.

This biblical wisdom is embodied in humble, substantive elders who are imperfect and limited and yet trust God. This wisdom is anchored in vital faith, lived in response to God's gifts of life and promises, and embodied in a great many faithful elders in the history of God's people.

Major elements of this robust biblical view of wisdom were present among many of the twenty-first-century elders interviewed. Not only was wisdom present in their lives, these elders were being called upon to exercise their wisdom in their communities. One can especially see these attributes of wisdom at work in Eric, who is known in his communities as *E*.

Eric: Wise Community Elder

Eric is eighty-three and a much celebrated and respected public servant and civil rights leader among the generations in his city and state. While he no longer holds public office, Eric continues to be a force in public life, serving on nonprofit boards, teaching continuing-education courses at a local university, leading at his church, and joining conversations with young civil servants and advocates regarding their public responsibilities.

Eric had a distinguished career in public service at local and state levels. He was a secondary-school teacher, college professor, social worker, and institute fellow. He was executive director of a nonprofit community center and of an urban coalition at critical junctures in their development. Later, he was an ombudsman for corrections, a public-housing director, and active in the Rainbow Coalition. Eric continues advocacy work as a senior conversant in these organizations' ongoing issues. Eric recently taught a course at a local university on race and culture.

Eric continues to utilize his access to intersections of policy discussion and power by participating in "generational networks," passing on his knowledge and experience to those in the two generations younger than he. Eric speaks of "the importance of investing in community" and understanding the impact of "globalization yet remaining connected to a particular place." To this end, in 2011 he participated in an oral-history project that critically examined the past while keeping an eye toward implications for the present and the future.

Eric reads voraciously, especially current newspapers and biographies. He says, "I watch news television, surfing channels so I can get diverse points of view."

Eric grew up in the segregated South. He remembers that "as a young person I had an imagination about what life could be, and my dreaming became a constructive way to handle oppression. I moved from the South to the Northeast, where I was still a distinct minority. I learned that my mere presence changed the dynamics of groups and situations." In the Northeast, Eric had an influential teacher who, although white, introduced him to black authors.

Eric asserts, "I believe in the *power of one*, for as a minority person my very presence makes a difference, and my voice makes an even greater difference."

Eric has two sons and a daughter and six grandchildren. He is in communication with someone in his family on a daily basis. Eric is proud of his family. He reflects on their progress over the years: "Third generation out of slavery, members of my family are strong people, well-embedded in American culture and economic capacity. I celebrate this progress, strength, and accomplishment."

Eric values the notion of the *messy table*. He says, "I want to help this generation of leaders broaden and expand who is in the important conversations so that people are not talking just with like-minded persons or missing key voices." Eric believes in the importance of institutional connections. He asserts, "The key is that people can't walk away but must stay in the dialogue."

Eric is a living historian. He is grounded in his belief in a gracious and righteous God who is alive and working justice through, among other venues, the Christian church. Eric brings both reflected experience and an informed presence to that church and to the world. He brings catalytic questions, has an extensive network of influential relationships, and is an important mentor of younger generations, especially young African Americans both in the church and in the community.

Eric is mentally active and engaged. He is a spirited activist and catalytic question poser, a current Christian walking in the "tradition and spirit and wisdom" of biblical elders.

Blessing

> All these are the twelve tribes of Israel, and this is what their father said to them when he blessed them, blessing each one of them with a suitable blessing. (Gen 49:28)

> When Jacob ended his charge to his sons, he drew up his feet into the bed, breathed his last, and was gathered to his people. (Gen 49:33)

In the Old Testament, old age and dying were the occasions for passing a blessing to the next generation. In Israel, the blessing by a family elder was a milestone event in which God's blessing of Israel to be a blessing to all nations was passed from generation to generation. It was also the occasion when the family was to be unified in this profound mission. One can see this blessing at work in Jacob, who at the end of his life acts very differently than his father, Isaac. Isaac had passed on this blessing to only one of his sons, the younger one who deceived him, thus creating division and alienation in the family. Unlike his father, Jacob blessed each of his sons, thus unifying a conflicted family and confirming for each family member God's call and their place in Israel's mission to bless the world.

For Christian families today, who in Christ have been "blessed to be blessing," similar challenges emerge. What does "blessing the world God loves" look like today? How does a Christian family develop an identity and vision of being "blessed to be a blessing?" How does a matriarch or patriarch participate in passing such a mission on to the next generation? In the Isaac/Esau/Jacob/Joseph story of three generations of blessing, there are clues about how to and how not to pass on the blessing. What might it look like for elders in the family to describe the realities of this calling to be a blessing to others and to be intentional, authentic, and direct in passing this calling on to the next generations?

Simeon and Anna

Luke's Gospel records moments in the lives of two wise and devout elders who, during Roman occupation of their nation, stand at the continuation of God's work with Israel in the mission of Jesus, which in turn gives rise to the mission of the Christian church.

The Spirit rests on Simeon, a righteous and devout elder. The Spirit reveals to Simeon that he will not die until he has met Israel's Messiah, so he is on the lookout for God's promised one who will rescue Simeon's people. Simeon knows Israel's law and prophets, and he knows Isaiah's prophecy of the coming of the Messiah. His knowledge of the tradition, his practice of prayer, and his "waiting on the Spirit" bring him to the temple in Jerusalem on the day of Jesus's presentation. Simeon recognizes Jesus as the Messiah and expresses his praise to God. Simeon takes Jesus in his arms and praises God, saying,

> Master, now you are dismissing your servant in peace, according to your word; for my eyes have seen your salvation, which you have prepared in the presence of all peoples, a light for revelation to the Gentiles and for glory to your people Israel. (Luke 2:29–32)

His prayer expands the vision of God's mission. In this Christ child, all peoples—both Jews and gentiles—will be included in the salvation story of God. Simeon's pronouncement is not only heard by Jesus and his parents, but his words are taken up and echoed through the centuries as an acclamation of God's saving presence and action on behalf of God's people everywhere.

Anna is a widow and a prophetess in her eighties. The daughter of Phanuel of the tribe of Asher, she fasts and worships at the temple night and day. When Jesus is presented at the temple and Simeon is affirming Jesus's identity as the salvation and light of all peoples—a radical new expression of God's reign of grace in the world—Anna praises God and speaks of God's coming to all who are wondering and waiting for the liberation and enlightenment of their nation. Anna becomes one of the first Christian witnesses and evangelists.

Along with shepherds and angels, Simeon and Anna, wise male and female elders representing the tribes and traditions and prophets of Israel, all confirm Jesus's identity as Messiah, give thanks for God's ongoing action, and broadcast Jesus's arrival to those waiting to know. So, too, comes the call to contemporary elders to bear witness to the presence of Christ in their lives over time and throughout their world—to carry Christian witness across the bridge from one generation to another.

Reconciled with God and Called to Serve

Christians believe that God in Jesus Christ entered a broken world whose inhabitants are alienated from God and one another so that the broken, alienated world and all that are in it might have life and have it more abundantly. Because God loves the world, God continues to act in Jesus's life, death, and resurrection to rescue, reconcile, and restore the world and all human beings, including elders. In baptism, all Christians—elders included—are claimed by God and endowed with the benefits of Christ's death and resurrection.

In baptism, God rescues, reconciles, and restores Christians and sets them free. And God calls these baptized to live so that the world God loves might thrive—elders included. Grateful for God's saving gifts, elders are called to live graciously so that they, their family and friends, their communities, their churches, and their world might thrive. Elders are to ask: How do I act so that I and those in God's world might live well?

In all their relationships and in all those places where they carry out their lives, elders can be called into this mission. As they do so, they are to pick up the responsibility God gave them at the beginnings of humankind, including stewarding the creation, or as one elder says, "getting to work and managing the planet." These responsibilities become concrete and active in daily life. Elder's lives matter to God and to the life of the world. Some elders will live out callings that are similar to those of earlier life stages, while other elders will serve in new ways, particularly unique to the life stage of elderhood. Some elders will choose their serving roles, while others will have servant roles thrust upon them by circumstances and by other people. Some may experience surprising calls.

> God calls these baptized to live so that the world God loves might thrive—elders included.

Sarah, one of the elders interviewed, understands the nuances of these callings. She sees the importance of her life as being "in the little things I can do for others to make their life better. I believe that the smallest thing I can do today is important to God and to others." She says, "When I wonder, 'What is life beyond eighty for?' I imagine it may be in these small things that I can still do for others." Joyce Ann Mercer, a Christian educator, takes this notion even further. She writes, "if vocation is about God's call to persons (and communities) claiming them across the whole of their lives, surely God calls older adults amid all their differences within the time of older adulthood, to vocations of service and love too. . . . We find older adult vocation particularly emphasizing *who* we are as creatures of God, *how* we are in relationship (with God, with others), and *what* capacities we evoke in others, rather than what we produce or accomplish."[2]

Elders and Gifts of the Spirit

In the New Testament, all believers drawn by the Spirit into faith in Jesus Christ and baptized into his body are called to participate in building up the whole body of Christ through the grace God extends to them by exercising the gift(s) they have been given. Each person, young and old, is called "for the work of ministry, for building up the body of Christ, until all of us come to the unity of the faith and of the knowledge of the Son of God, to maturity, to the full stature of Christ" (Eph 4:12–13). Elders, too, are called to discern their spiritual gifts and imagine how to use them to equip other Christians and to grow the current expressions of Christ's body, the church.

So what gifts might elders possess? The lists provided in Ephesians 4:11 and 1 Corinthians 12:28 are places to start. They include being apostles, prophets, evangelists, pastors, and teachers; deeds of power; healing; assistance; leadership; and speaking in tongues. Nothing is said about any of these gifts being withheld from elders. Across the years, the Christian church has discovered these gifts in a great many elders and greatly benefited from elders exercising these gifts. We think of giants of the faith such as Desmond Tutu and Mother Teresa, but we see the gifts at work in everyday elders. Consider Jane's story.

Jane: Prayer Warrior

Jane's latest period of life is marked by her husband's death and her serious physical decline. She is experiencing multiple maladies: loss of hearing, failing eye sight, trembling hands, and limited energy. At age eighty-four, Jane laments, "These physical limitations have greatly restricted my mobility and lessened my capacity to care for myself and my daily needs." All of these losses, Jane says, "remind me of the loss of my son to alcoholism." Because of the 2008 stock-market decline, Jane has also experienced a decade of significant financial struggle. A reverse mortgage on her home has provided just enough money to meet expenses.

Nevertheless, Jane's life is not defined by her losses. She speaks of a transformative relationship with God that is the "core of her existence and continues to grow." Jane says, "My life is wrapped in a sense of gratitude for God's gracious care and providence." So, Jane is free to invest her life in God's mission and ministry. She has discovered her spiritual gift is intercessory prayer; as Jane puts it: "I am a prayer warrior!" She "does her prayers" before she arises in the morning, and she "does her prayers" before she goes to bed at night. She leads a prayer group at her church that prays for the world, the community, the congregation, each other, and the long list of persons who ask for their prayers. Jane is spiritually gifted at praying, bringing God's presence and actions to bear in the lives of countless individuals and setting a "spiritually expectant tone" for her entire congregation.

Vulnerability and Decline

Christians are realists, thoroughly aware of the limits and downside of the human condition. Whether referencing their own experience, scientific findings, or the Bible, the elders I interviewed knew that joints ache and break down, that physical decline is inherent in the human life cycle, and that "flesh is like grass that is here today and gone tomorrow."

This cycle of aging is chronicled in the sciences as well as in Scripture. Anabolism (the building up of the cells and metabolism of the human body) and catabolism (the breaking down of the cells and metabolism of the human body) are natural, normal, and essential dimensions of the ongoing organic flow of life. Greater amounts of anabolism occur during childhood; greater amounts of catabolism occur during elderhood. This later phenomenon is referred to as senescence, or biological aging, and is present in human cells and organisms in varying forms and at varying times. These biological processes are accompanied by psychological and existential dynamics as well. Addressing the implications of these differences and processes, Carl Jung writes, "It is impossible to live through the evening of life in accordance with the programs appropriate for the morning, since what has great importance then will have little now, and the truth of the morning will be the error of the evening."[3] While not using biological or anthropological scientific terms, Scripture asserts it is good and right to accept and tend the uniqueness of each season of life with knowledge and wisdom. Physical birth and, with it, much of human development are natural phenomena, just as are physical decline and death. From this, critical questions emerge: How does a child rise up well? How does an elder decline and die well?

The poet in Ecclesiastes asserts, "There is a time to be born and a time to die" (3:2). It seems that Ecclesiastes is referencing the early ascendency and the later decline of the human life cycle. There is birthing time. There is dying time. If one knows something of human beginnings and endings, how does one participate well in the birthing and the dying? Scripture and Christian tradition provide clues.

In Scripture and Christian tradition, we do not attribute disaster, accident, illness, and disease to God. Rather, we recognize that pain and loss are a part of human existence and may at times emanate from another power that seeks to destroy life and infuse pain and suffering. We seek to fight disease, heal injury, or cure illnesses while at the same time we need to accompany someone in their dying or living well until they die.

While recognizing and accepting nature's limit on human life expectancy, the Scriptures also stand over against illness and disease as well as promote human healing and wellness. Jesus's ministry stands out. His miracles of healing are a major dimension of his bringing the kingdom of God on earth. Jesus's acts of healing and restoring people, young and old, to health are signs of God's reign. The sick are healed. The lame or "crippled from birth" are healed. Lepers are healed. Those who have prematurely died are raised and healed. Accident, illness, and disease are dimensions of evil and the evil one, which stand over and against Jesus's mission of bringing abundant life. Jesus opposes them vigorously and expansively.

The elders interviewed in this study were all "living the natural human decline" of elderhood, even as they fought and endured in the face of injury, illness, and disease. One can see this struggle in Burt and with Joan.

Burt is ninety-two and in generally good health. He is energetic and sharp mentally, though he has "endured and survived" multiple diseases. He is currently "moving about more slowly" and "having to work to concentrate." Burt exhibits significant physical and mental decline as he "journeys toward the ever-narrowing place" of death. Yet to get to his present "gracious place" in his decline, Burt says, "Leukemia, skin cancer, prostate cancer, and pneumonia have come and battered my life, but through the powers of modern medicine, my strong will, and my supportive communities, each illness has been overcome." Burt is resilient, a survivor of multiple illnesses and diseases, and yet he most certainly lives adaptively with the physical and mental decline that come with aging.

Joan, age seventy-four, had a stroke at age forty-nine that left her unable to balance or care for herself. For twenty years, her husband has been her primary caregiver. This altered relationship has deepened and expanded their marriage while mentally and spiritually strengthening both Joan and her husband, Frank. They have faced and compensated for the residual effects of Joan's stroke and, in doing so, have mutually enriched each other's lives and become an inspiration to other couples, most especially to their friends and acquaintances. Joan and Frank have imaginatively adapted to Joan's handicap and have been strengthened by its challenges, while at the same time they have experienced the limits of decline that come with aging.

> People who live by faith do not escape the messiness and vulnerabilities associated with aging.

People who live by faith do not escape the messiness and vulnerabilities associated with aging. They experience the natural decline of physical and mental powers just like anyone else. But it seems those who have faith and who are part of a faith community are able to show a resilience that is born of hope and buoyed by the support provided by people in their faith communities.

Prelude and Bridge to Life Forever

There is a radically disruptive Christian promise that profoundly influenced many of the elders interviewed and most certainly shapes elderhood:

> For I am convinced that neither death, nor life, nor angels, nor rulers, nor things present, nor things to come, nor powers, nor height, nor depth, nor anything else in all creation, will be able to separate us from the love of God in Christ Jesus. (Rom 8:38–39)

I am the resurrection and the life. Those who believe in
me, even though they die, will live. (John 11:25)

The promises above add new dimension to our understanding of
the human lifetime and give new meaning to one's last chapter.
How does one live when elderhood is not the end, when elderhood and its stages, and death itself, are rather moments of transition into a fuller life with God and God's people forever? What
are the implications of these promises? How do they influence
the quality of life for Christian elders?

One important implication is that death, elderhood's natural termination, is not the final word on human life nor life's
final chapter; rather death is a doorway to a new life. Baptized
into Christ's death and resurrection, Christian elders live in the
promise of resurrection and life forever. One of the interviewees
exclaims, "The end has been kicked out of our casket; we are on
the threshold of better life and a better place."

Elders exist in two experiences of *time* that are distinctly different. Their present chronological time is relatively short, but
their "future time in the new heavens and new earth" is forever.
As elders are closing down an earthly journey, they are passing
into another time, another expression of transformed human
existence. Many of the elders interviewed recognized that they
were making this journey. Consider Gail, Ron, and Dee.

Gail: Finishing Strong and Getting Ready to Die

Gail is now seventy-eight. Her pathway into elderhood was
set off by her kids leaving home and by her going to work. At

her new employment, Gail developed accounting skills that equipped her for significant positions in two major companies. Although now retired from that work, she continues to utilize the expertise and experience she gained in her employment to manage her family's rental properties. Gail continues to learn; she belongs to an investment club that informs her family's investment planning.

Gail is in good health. She walks in the mornings and eats well, but her husband Les's health concerns have claimed her attention. In spite of her husband's many health challenges, she is grateful: "Les has survived lymphoma, prostate cancer, and skin cancer with much good medical care, a positive attitude, and strong support from our friends and faith community."

Gail and Les have also been deeply impacted by Les's close friend taking his life after being diagnosed with dementia. The friend left a note telling his family he loved them and didn't want to be a burden on them and society. This situation has caused Gail and Les to start thinking about the end of their lives. Gail reflects, "We had lived as if we weren't going to die; the big change is realizing that we are, and we have begun to make arrangements for our deaths. We have moved from our big house on a lake to a quality retirement community. We've dedicated our bodies to the university for research, to be returned to the family after cremation and then buried in a military cemetery." Gail and Les are presently participants in an experimental health-initiatives study; they want the ends of their lives here to matter even as they go on to another life yet to come.

Ron and Dee: Walking into the Future Together

Ron and Dee are, as they put it, "walking into the future together." They regularly talk through making plans for when they die, as well as plans for "living fully" in their journey "toward a narrow and restricted place before they are set free forever." In response to these conversations, Ron and Dee have refurbished their home so they can stay there and be cared for until they die. They have purchased burial plots and planned their funerals. They have spoken with their children about these plans and updated their will most specifically to reflect the different financial situations of their children. They are getting ready for the transition. All the while, their faith and its practiced spirituality are central in their lives. Prayer for Ron and music for Dee are real day-to-day communications with the God they know and love now, and whom they trust will meet them on the other side.

Faith's Foundations for Elderhood

This exploration of faith and faith communities, and their explicit and implicit influence in the lives of the elders interviewed, reveals foundational glimpses of a rich and hope-filled framework and portrait of older adulthood. In this Christian understanding and view of elderhood, older adults are

- Endowed with dignity through birth and baptism
- Responsible for "co-managing the earth" in their own time and place

- Called to be storytellers and tradition bearers of God's presence and action
- Conveyors of wisdom and mentors of the young
- Claimed and called by God to serve their neighbors and the world
- Spiritually gifted to equip others and build up the body of Christ, the church
- Gathered, enlightened, and sustained as members of the community of faith
- Recognize they are vulnerable, fragile, and on a short journey to death
- Promised abundant eternal life and are on the way to a new life with God

In this view of older adults, elderhood is distinctive and filled with change and promise. Scripture paints a realistic portrait of respected, able elders who are called to serve God and neighbor even as they experience life's pain and vulnerabilities. The same can be said of faith-filled elders today. They are forward-looking pilgrims ready to cross over to the beginnings of whole and full life that goes on forever!

The Christian faith powerfully undergirds the promise of elderhood, of a third, transitional

> Scripture paints a realistic portrait of respected, able elders who are called to serve God and neighbor even as they experience life's pain and vulnerabilities.

productive chapter of the human life cycle. Not only is this good news for twenty-first-century elders, it is good news for faith communities as well. Congregations can turn to faithful elders for hope, inspiration, and strength. Rather than simply lamenting the growing numbers of elders in their midst, communities of faith can actively draw on their wisdom and deep faith. And they can function as Centers for Vital and Resilient Aging. The age wave and the capacities of elders should be seen as an asset to all communities of faith. In wisdom and by faith, elders are rising.

Exploration and Discussion

1. The Scriptures value wisdom highly. They provide examples of wise elders leading God's people and describe wisdom as:

   - The fear (or honoring) of God
   - Recognition of God's power and holiness
   - Belief in God's authority
   - Genuine response to God's gracious love and gifts of love and salvation
   - Informed by studying the law and the prophets
   - Living morally—doing the right thing
   - Reflecting on and learning from the past, especially one's mistakes, and investing these learnings in the enhancement of the present and future

Name elders you know who look and act like this. What makes them wise? How does your life display such wisdom? How can the enacting of wisdom become a vocation for elders? How can congregations equip wise elders and tap into their wisdom?

2. Elders who describe themselves as people of faith are not spared life's messiness or perils. Like everyone else, they experience physical pain, illness, and disease. The Gospels report Jesus healing many people. His actions provide the promise of hope and wholeness. Today, we recognize the many miraculous ways physical ailments and illnesses can be rigorously treated and healed. How do you think about healing in your life and the lives of others? Declining health is a natural part of life. Should this prevent us from rigorously treating illness and disease? Why or why not?

3. Which of the following callings resonate with you most? Why?

  - Responsibly caring for the earth
  - Telling the story of God's presence and action
  - Mentoring the young
  - Serving my neighbor
  - Using my gifts to equip others and to build up my faith community
  - Gathering others in community
  - Offering prayers of health and comfort

How do you think congregations can better enable elders to express their callings?

4. One of the elders on what her faith community means to her and her husband: "Our congregation combines our most significant friendships with a sense of purpose through the mission work we do together; our faith community is the social and spiritual center of our lives." Do you belong to a church or some kind of faith community? If so, how would you describe the place it holds in your life?

3

Elderhood:
A New Life Stage

The 20th century is over, and most solutions to 20th century aging don't work anymore. . . . What is the new purpose for maturity?

—Ken Dychtwald[1]

How are we to understand the advancing age wave and this new era of aging? I noticed in the responses of the elders interviewed that Scripture and the Christian tradition were hugely influential. Might these provide perspectives and guidance for old age in a time of significantly different character and circumstances? Might science and folk wisdom make generative contributions? Might there be combinations of concepts and understandings that capture, on the one hand, the commonalities of this stage of life and, on the other hand, accurately express the particularities and complexities of its distinct phases? While adults from sixty-seven to ninety-seven are all elders and have much in common, their lives are majorly different. Adding to the complexity, to a certain extent, individuals each age in their own way.

There is much discussion presently regarding old age or older adulthood and when it begins. Some gerontologists claim it is "Adulthood II," the last of four periods of life.[2] Others speak of older adulthood as three periods with two transitions. There is little agreement about what constitutes these periods and what to call them, or even when old age begins. In a 2009 Pew study, Americans gave thirteen different responses to the phrase "a person is old when she or he _____". Responses included:

- Turns eighty-five
- Can't live independently
- Can't drive a car
- Turns seventy-five
- Frequently forgets familiar names
- Finds their health is failing
- Has trouble walking up stairs
- Has bladder-control problems
- Is no longer sexually active
- Turns sixty-five
- Retires from work
- Has grandchildren
- Has gray hair[3]

Some who study generations, especially those who work closely with marketing, don't like terms or concepts that describe persons in the last third of life as *old*, especially stereotypically, as in elderly, aged, senior citizens, or retirees. Neither do many older adults. Laura Carstensen, psychology professor at Stanford, likes the term *perennials*. She writes, "The symbolism it connotes is perfect. For one, 'perennials' makes clear that we're still here, blossoming again and again. It also suggests a new model of life in which people engage and take breaks, making new starts repeatedly. Perennials aren't guaranteed to blossom year after year, but given proper conditions, good soil and nutrients, they can go on for decades. It's aspirational."[4]

Older Adults' Commonalities

The older adults I interviewed are in their sixties, seventies, eighties, and nineties. I discovered these elders who represent a span of thirty years have common characteristics. While every one of them is aging in their own way, they all are experiencing variations of the physical changes that come with aging. They all share certain freedoms, such as not spending full time earning a living. They all have significant amounts of discretionary time and attention. They are tapping their wisdom, as well as their lifetime experience and life-reflected knowledge and skill, to make contributions to their communities. Whether they are repairing houses, providing financial counsel, caring for the dying, tending families, or writing books on loss, their roles are substantive. They are reinventing themselves as they adapt to and compensate for the changes in their societal roles and in their physical and mental capacities. They are aware of the importance of *shedding*, or reducing the stuff in their lives. They are experiencing losses that come with the social, physical, mental, financial, and spiritual dynamics of being society's oldest generations. They are all navigating a long, unique stage of the human life cycle.

Elders and Elderhood: Three Distinct Periods

Based on the discoveries I made among the fifty-three interviewees and based on my understanding of Scripture and the Christian tradition, I propose that the concepts of *elder* and *elderhood* are able to capture and describe the commonalities of this prolonged time of life. Further, I propose that this three-decade-long life stage comprises three distinct periods: early elderhood, middle elderhood and late elderhood.

> This three-decade-long life stage comprises three distinct periods: early elderhood, middle elderhood and late elderhood.

Resurrecting the notion of elder, and expanding elder to elderhood as a distinct, significant tri-period stage of life with its own character, purposes, and tasks is challenging given our culture's historical proclivity for youthfulness and its negative portrayal of the frailness associated with being *elderly*. There is, however, strong contextual, historical, and biblical warrant for using the terms *elder* and *elderhood*.

In hunting-and-gathering societies, and agrarian societies as well, elders are uniquely able contributors to familial and tribal well-being. Even as elders' physical strength and energy diminish, their accumulated experience, reflected knowledge and seasoned understandings of their culture's stories and traditions are essential to familial and communal resilience and vitality. Given these valuable capacities, and freed from producing food, clothing, and shelter, elders become children's teachers, young adults' mentors, and family, tribal, and community mentors, adjudicators, and sages. This was the case in the Old Testament's portrayal of an elder's role in ancient Israel. While not all older people were considered elders, the capable and engaged older men and women were respected for their wisdom and societal contributions rather than dismissed or denigrated for their lack of youthfulness and physical prowess. *Elder* was not only common, descriptive language for an older adult, this term carried the sense of the older adult's great value and expressed their culture's respect for them. I propose that the expanding presence and strategic contributions of today's older adults might well be captured by resurrecting these terms and drawing on their substantive historical meanings.

The resurrection and reconstitution of *elder* is also an important corrective. The Industrial Revolution relied on science and commerce as the primary informants and drivers of society. In the industrial age, intellectual disciplines and scientific discoveries generated new information and innovation that focused on the present and future. Experiments led to new learning, which generated new ideas and quickly transformed them into action and production. This demanded great human energy and imagination. Production, distribution, and consumption of goods in turn provided earning power that translated into purchasing food, clothing, shelter, and much, much more. The past and the past's traditions were not only considered outdated, they were often viewed as roadblocks to a better future. The *new* and the *young* became societies' models and heroes. To be energetic and risk-taking as well as youthfully beautiful became the personal and societal norms and the traits highly sought after. The momentum and force of this new age held little value for and saw nothing essential in older folks' knowledge and reflected experience. Elders weren't needed. Moreover, they didn't look like the *model human* nor did they have the model human's energy and physical prowess. Elders were perceived as wrinkled and tired. Older adults were deemed unattractive, useless, often marginalized, considered a burden for society to take care of.

In spite of the industrial age's dismissal and detrimental stereotyping of seniors, much of its scientific discoveries and economic prowess contributed greatly to older adulthood's improved health, greater financial security, and better quality of life. New medicines, body-part replacements, sophisticated mobility devices, better financial plans, and expanded social-support systems laid the foundations for the dawning of a new era for older adults.

Elderhood in the Information Age

Enter the digital revolution, driven by information communicated quickly, expansively, and inexpensively. In the ensuing information age, data, ideas, pictures, stories, opinions, and so on can be generated and sent across the globe instantly. Older adults, along with everyone else, have access and the ability to disseminate and receive information anytime, anywhere. In such a world, information is power. One needn't look young, be mobile, or be enfranchised by a particular group to participate. Anyone who has the inclination, the time, the capacity to write, an opinion or idea or story to tell, and a devise connected to the internet can be a player.

Seniors are indeed players on the internet and social media. Seventy-six percent of Americans age fifty and older have a digital media device (cell phone, computer, or tablet) and these numbers are increasing each year.[5] Intrigued and drawn to the capacities and possibilities of the internet and social media, greater numbers of elders are participants in larger societal enterprises. Employing their minds and their fingers, elders can participate in extended families, friendships, online affinity groups, blogs, and Twitter, and, through a plethora of apps, engage and manipulate communication and influence everything from intimate private exchanges to global public policy.

With significant discretionary time, much reflected experience, lively passion, and no lack of ideas and opinions, elders have more fully reentered the worlds of family, neighborhood, community, education, commerce, politics, religion, and leisure in large numbers and with significant impact. In this emerging engagement, elders can have expansive influence and gravitas similar to that of elders in societies prior to the Industrial Revolution. As we noted earlier, they can live out the scriptural understanding of elders as engaged providers of wisdom and witness. In the information age, elders are increasingly present, engaged, and influential. Elders are rising.

One can see the commonalities of this life stage and the distinct differences of its periods in John, an early elder, Frankie, a middle elder, and Pete and Stephanie, late elders.

John: Early Elder

John, age seventy-two, has been retired fifteen years following a productive career as an electrical engineer with a major airline manufacturer. Retirement provided John the freedom to choose what he wanted to do with his time and attention. Because balance is important in John's life, retirement has been an opportunity to develop his own rhythms of relationships and activities. John is constructing an ever-changing life matrix of family, church, friends, and volunteering.

In this emerging engagement, elders can have expansive influence and gravitas similar to that of elders in societies prior to the Industrial Revolution.

John says of his present life: "I'm grateful. I came from a family of means. I have been successful professionally and financially. I own a fifty-seven-foot yacht. I've been blessed, and it motivates me to care for others." John and his yacht have become an effective ministry at his church; he takes groups on retreats, fishing trips, and service projects.

John is passionate and multitalented. He's a people person. He says, "Touching people's lives is important and meaningful to me." John's a problem solver; he especially enjoys working with others to address community issues. He chuckles as he tells me, "My satisfaction is in moving a project from idea to completion." As an engineer in management, John learned "how to make things happen . . . [to] go where the needs are . . . [to] work with the pieces of the system . . . [to] get people together to make decisions and get to work."

John's a thinker. He philosophizes, "People were created to live interdependently. We're built for relationships; our life is what we share with each other. In the beginning, we are taken care of; then we can care for others. Then there comes a day when we will be taken care of again."

Friends contribute greatly to John's life; his long-standing friendships are treasured. John says reflectively, "discernment around ongoing challenges and questions is critical to the quality of my life; I do this through talking matters through with my friends."

Scouting is a family tradition—John and his father were Eagle Scouts, and John's son and grandson are in Scouts.

John is also a church leader who has been chairperson of his congregation. Presently, he is the leader of Grace in Action, a group at his church organized to respond to needs of the community. They fix houses, work with people in financial crises, do maintenance, troubleshoot faulty appliances, and more.

John is healthy and physically fit, though not as energetic as he remembers he once was. He still volunteers doing physical work constructing houses, repairing buildings, and refurbishing landscapes.

At seventy-two, John is downsizing. He says, "we're moving from a very large home to a smaller one; we're shedding some of what we own. I don't want our children to have to dispense with our stuff; I don't want to leave them with a burden." John and his wife recently purchased long-term care insurance and told their children so. He is reworking his will to reflect the realities of his and his wife Sarah's present stages of life and situations.

Frankie: Middle Elder

Frankie is eighty. A career nurse, during retirement Frankie has "carried over her nursing to giving care" to persons around her. Frankie was the primary caregiver when her sister was dying. She was one of her mother's caregivers when her mother died. She cared for a man she was engaged to, who died before they could marry. She later married, and she cared for her husband for six years before he died one year ago. Caregiving and loss are major recurring aspects of Frankie's life.

While Frankie has experienced multiple losses, two of them have been especially difficult. These two losses are different from each other, but equally devastating. One is the death of her husband, who was a great companion, community leader, and successful businessman. The other loss is her son becoming an agnostic; Frankie speaks of this as her "biggest disappointment."

The latest period in Frankie's life is marked by the death of her husband. Frankie says, "Day to day, life is up and down. I go to church and cry often; I force myself to go out." Agile and energetic at eighty, Frankie is a tennis player, and she claims "it what's gotten me through."

Frankie had three sons before she divorced at midlife. These three sons and their families are important to her. Because she is not in close proximity to her children and grandchildren, digital communication greatly enriches her day-to-day connections with them and is key to staying in touch. Frankie thinks back to last summer and exclaims, "our major family celebration July 4 was the best."

So now Frankie has to decide where to live and in what setting. She's originally from Massachusetts, where her sons and their families live. She is also drawn to New England because, she says, "I'm a Patriot's fan." For a long time, Frankie has been living in the South, first with her husband and now alone. In her Southern home, she has made close friends who are her day-to-day support and companions. And her church is nearby. So Frankie is torn between being with her family or being with her friends. She realizes she is slowing down, and she will soon need people to watch out for her even as she has cared for others. So, she ponders, "where should I live now and in what kind of housing?" It's difficult; she hasn't decided.

Peter and Stephanie: Late Elders

Stephanie and Peter are both ninety-two and have been married sixty-eight years. They reside in a care community, except during the winter months, which they spend, assisted by in-home caregivers, in a condo in the South. This is their third living arrangement during retirement.

Stephanie and Peter understand themselves to be a team in family, profession, and life. Their teamwork extends even to their adaption to their cognitive impairment. One of them has short-term memory loss, yet good long-term memory; the other's long-term memory is sketchy and short-term memory strong. So Stephanie and Peter seamlessly fill in the gaps from each other's memory losses.

Stephanie is a gracious, quiet, good listener. She says of herself, "I am a thankful care receiver, even though I don't like to ask for help." Stephanie has difficulty with the regular everyday functions of getting dressed, making meals, and remembering her daily schedule. She says, "getting through the day's basics takes up most of my time." Once energized by travel, Stephanie no longer likes to go to new places, given her present limitations. Stephanie is okay physically, but fragile. While she can focus on the present and carry on normal conversation, she often gets confused, especially with time and numbers.

Peter is spirited and articulate. He first retired at age sixty-eight. During his "retirement," he has worked several short-term full-time and part-time positions. During his eighty-ninth and ninetieth years, he wrote a book. Peter says, "my lifetime pastoral role remains central to my self-understanding."

Peter has had two subdural hematomas and two brain surgeries. He has significant hearing loss. His decaying teeth have required the installation of oral plates. Peter has difficulty with balance; he fell four times last year. He stopped driving at age ninety-one.

Family is important to Stephanie and Peter. They had two brilliant sons. One son is a successful businessman who, along with his wife, "watch over us," says Peter. Their other son, Jack, was a Yale professor who died in his forties of AIDS. Stephanie and Peter have seven grandchildren, five of whom they learned about via a letter from Jack's daughter, whom they didn't know existed.

Faith and faith communities are constitutive for Peter and Stephanie. They have strong bonds with worshipping communities in their two residential locations in the South and the upper Midwest.

Elderhood's Distinct Periods

While John, Frankie, Peter, and Stephanie share many of the common characteristics of aging, John in his seventies, Frankie in her eighties, and Peter and Stephanie in their nineties, represent differing periods of elderhood. John's robust life of leadership, community activism, and construction is different from Frankie's dedicated and resilient life of caregiving, struggle with multiple losses, slowing down, and inner conflict about where to live. Both John's and Frankie's lives are different than Peter and Stephanie's adaptive, collaborative life of compensation for cognitive limitations and their graciousness and hopefulness around the basics of daily existence. John in early elderhood, Frankie in middle elderhood, and

Peter and Stephanie in late elderhood are at differing places on the aging journey, places that have their own particular characteristics.

One of the interviewees informally and humorously characterizes these three differing periods as "go-go, slow-go, and no-go."

So, what defines and characterizes early, middle, or late elderhood? Does age? Does activity? Does relative physical or cognitive health? Do degrees of independence? While no one factor determines a period's onset or essential character, a combination of factors regularly marks the transitions and a particular period's common elder orientation and lifestyle. One can see these dynamics at work across time in Cheryl and Ralph's twenty-four years of retirement.

Cheryl and Ralph: Three Rhythms of Elderhood

Cheryl and Ralph's twenty-four-year retirement has displayed distinct rhythms within three periods. The first ten-year segment was fast-paced, filled with the operation of a bed-and-breakfast and gift shop. They much enjoyed meeting and serving people and have many friends whom they initially met as their clients.

The next ten years were spent split between summers in the Midwest and winters in the South. These years were filled with volunteering, travel, and assisting in the raising of their grandkids.

In this latest period, their daily schedules are more open and slower paced, or as Ralph says, "We've entered a calmer time of more being than doing. It's great to have a 2:00 p.m. coffee date with Cheryl every day." This calmer time fits well with their present physical challenges, as Ralph has had a knee replaced and will have the other replaced soon; he has also had surgery removing cancerous tissue from his face. Cheryl has also undergone surgery.

During this calmer time, digital communication has become more prominent in Cheryl's and Ralph's lives. What with moving back and forth each year between the Midwest and the South, as well as stepping back from much of the schedule of grandchildren's events and having more time to read, Cheryl and Ralph each have a cell phone, a tablet, and a laptop computer that they use for family communication, reading, and learning.

Cheryl and Ralph have been intensely involved in their family and in their two congregations, one in the Midwest and one in the South. Even as they were purposefully and fully engaged in raising their two sons and daughter, they have also been significant contributors to their grandchildren's upbringing, especially during the second segment of their retirement. With their highly successful children heavily scheduled with work and community, Cheryl and Ralph have been "back-up family presence" at special events, on sick days, and at many educational and recreational excursions. One example of this intergenerational investment in raising good people is participation in the Boy Scouts. Ralph went with a grandson to a national Scout Jamboree.

Cheryl and Ralph are ardent "church people." They are extensively engaged in their church communities. Cheryl says,

"Our faith gives us something to identify with . . . we love the sermons and make great friends at church." Their study of Scripture and the Christian tradition is long-standing. They took the Bethel Bible Series together in their thirties, and they still go to Bible studies. Through their churches, they volunteer at community food programs. Ralph says, "Now that we have more time to give, we are looking forward to doing more."

All of this has enhanced and sustained Cheryl's curious, outgoing spirit. She carries with her throughout elderhood the lively, talkative personality that marked her early life. Ralph summarizes this time of life well for both him and Cheryl at age seventy-eight when he says, "The purposeful life is important to us. We get up early; we want to accomplish something each day."

These dynamics and transitions at work in Cheryl's and Ralph's older adult rhythms are even more prevalent across the fifty-three interviewees. In my observations, the following characteristics most often marked the three periods of elderhood discussed above.

Early Elderhood

- Winding down full-time or part-time compensated career or work
- Wrestling with the transitional dynamics of retirement
- Redefinition and revaluation of self
- Freedom to shift time and attention to selected or chosen relationships and activities
- Many hours volunteering, often in physically active forms

- Significant amount of caregiving for other elders
- Often grand-parenting
- Gradual but accelerating physical and cognitive decline
- Significant interest in and amounts of travel
- Often rigorous physical exercise
- Highly mobile
- Accelerating loss of family members and friends
- Often change in residence/location responding to climate, maintenance, or family
- Roughly ages sixty-five to seventy-four

Middle Elderhood

- Mostly retired from career of full-time, compensated work
- Freedom to shift time and attention to selected or chosen relationships and activities
- Volunteering important but often in less physically active forms
- Caregiving for others diminishing with advancing age
- Often grand-parenting; some great-grand-parenting
- Physical and cognitive decline, modified lifestyle, and required adaptive responses
- Develop one or more chronic diseases or injuries
- Travel continues but tapers off
- Low-impact exercise
- Mobility diminishes
- Greater accelerating loss of family members and friends
- Change in residence and location; often assisted living

- Significant changes in relationship network(s)
- Probability of dying increases
- Roughly ages seventy-five to eighty-four

Late Elderhood

- Most time and attention given to accomplishing basic life tasks
- Little if any compensated work
- Little volunteering; if so, sedentary
- Significant freedom but diminishing energy to give attention to family and friends
- Still greater accelerating loss of family members and friends
- Physical and cognitive decline accelerate and greatly modify lifestyle
- Development of and living with one or more chronic diseases increases
- Little caregiving; more care receiving
- Often grandparenting and great-grandparenting
- Very low-impact exercise
- Little to no travel
- Mobility greatly decreases
- Change in residence; often to assisted living
- Accelerating change in relationship network(s)
- Probability of dying greatly increases
- Roughly ages eighty-five and above

While the combination of these factors generated distinctly different elder life period orientations and lifestyles, the transitions between early, middle, and late elderhood did not often occur as dramatic shifts, but more often than not occurred gradually around these common factors.

Elderhood's Signature Dimensions

From the interviewees, I learned much of the shape and form of older adults' increased presence, engagement, and influence, and their distinctive, essential roles in society. I learned that these older adults are carrying on these distinctive, essential roles in spite of their vulnerability to accident, illness, and disease as well as the decline that comes with the natural processes of aging. The elements of the elders' stories in the study coalesced in clusters of experiences and characteristics that formed seven major dimensions that are uniquely present in varying degrees and define the robust three periods of this stage of life. The seven pervasive, defining dimensions I discovered among these elders include:

- Presence—The capacity to be with; to be available flexibly and readily in the here and now
- Relationships—That sustain and build up oneself and others
- Passion—Compelling interests that motivate deep commitment and caring
- Purpose—Participation in and contribution to what matters; making a real difference

- Power—The ability to influence; to accomplish significant essential societal functions
- Playfulness—Fun, humor, enjoyment, and leisure
- Peril—Multiple and progressive vulnerabilities (decline, illness, accident, etc.) are real

Interestingly, these seven life dimensions emerging from the stories of the fifty-three interviewees mirror much of the essential character of aging and elderhood in Scripture and the Christian tradition, as well as align with findings gerontologists are reporting in the scientific literature on aging. Over the last decade, scientists conducting biological, psychological, sociological, economic, political, and spiritual investigation of older adulthood have been discovering a long, distinctive developmental process at the end of the arc of human life that reflects many of the reemerging historic assets of older adulthood. The MacArthur Foundation Research Network on an Aging Society found that assets such as the following increase with age.

- Reflected experience
- Social values
- Mentorship
- Patience
- Storytelling
- Moral courage
- Wisdom
- Emotional regulation
- Flexible time
- Big-picture perspective
- Sense of humor
- Spiritual insight

Could it be that in the information age scientists are discovering a distinctive, late-adulthood stage of life that has essential contributions to make to society in the twenty-first century? Could it be that many of the understandings of the roles and contributions of elders in Scripture and Christian tradition, especially in faith transmission, are reemerging? It seems so. It seems we are living into a new era of aging, a new/old stage of life I call elderhood, with early, middle, and late periods. The fifty-three older adults I met appear to be among the older adults leading the way in establishing this re-formed stage of the human life cycle. They are elders rising.

Exploration and Discussion

1. One elder described human beings and their life cycle in this way: "People were created to live interdependently. We're built for relationships; our life is what we share with each other. In the beginning, we are taken care of; then we can care for others. Then there comes a day when we will be taken care of again." Do you find this to be an accurate expression of the human lifespan? What are the strengths and limitations of this point of view? What does this point of view say about elderhood?

2. I propose that elderhood is a twenty- to thirty-year culmination of the human life cycle. It is often characterized by variations of:

- Flexible time
- Moral courage
- Mental decline
- Ongoing change
- Volunteering
- Relocation(s)
- Less time earning a living
- Sense of humor
- A variety of losses
- Physical decline
- Storytelling

- Reduction of
  things
- Less energy
- Reflected
  experience
- Wisdom

- Shifts in roles
- Freedoms
- Spiritual transitions
- Tested knowledge
  and skill
- Seeking a legacy

Which of these descriptors of society's oldest generation do you find to be accurate in your own life? What is missing?

3. Review the proposed seven realistic and promising dimensions of elderhood listed on pp. 81–82 above. Which of these dimensions do you see at work in elderhood? Which of these dimensions are present in your life? Which, if any, of these dimensions do you wish were more present in your life? Why?

4

Presence: The Capacity to Accompany

I sit at the back of the church and get into conversations with young people. I like . . . accompanying, being in conversation. . . . I work to bring people together . . . to listen . . . to speak.

—Sherry, age eighty-one

I've worked with my grief by writing notes to those from whom I received sympathy cards at the time of my husband's death; I let them know that I pray for them. I have formed a community of persons praying for each other. This has led me to look outward; this has drawn me through my grief.

—Phyllis, age seventy-nine

Brigid Schulte, in her *New York Times* best seller, *Over-whelmed: Work, Love, and Play When No One Has the Time*,[1] describes the demands and time pressures of modern life. She writes of the impact of not having the time to "do it all," of both individuals and society being unable to be either physically or mentally present in the blur of all that's going on. Overwhelmed by work, family, community responsibilities, and processing constant streams of data, we lose much of our capacity to be really present to ourselves and others. Many of the elders interviewed referenced being on this treadmill during the first two thirds of their lives. One of the largest changes they spoke of in their present retirement or older adulthood was getting off this treadmill of demands on their time and attention.

Eric, an observant eighty-three-year-old elder I interviewed, speaks of "the power of being present . . . the power of one." As a minority, he has often noticed his very presence makes a difference. In speaking of his experiences as a minority, Eric also identifies one of the most prevalent and influential capacities of all the elders interviewed. These older adults *show up*; they invest their time and pay attention. Sometimes this investment means taking time to be "at home in their own skin" (i.e., attentive to themselves); sometimes it's being with their families; sometimes it's being with their friends; other times it's being with other elders in their homes or communities; still other times it's being with the young or the marginalized or the lonely, the hurting, or the dying. It's not that they are not active or engaged or even busy; it's more that they are utilizing their freedom to make choices about where and how much of their time and attention they spend, and with whom. These elders mostly delighted in this freedom and were intentionally and intensely investing their time and their attention—their presence. Equally as interesting and important, whenever these elders are with others, their presence makes a difference. Consider the dynamics and power of this presence at work in Alvin and through him in his rural community.

Alvin: Available Assistant Extraordinaire

Alvin has lived all of his eighty-one years in the same community. He knows everyone. He is a community fixture. Alvin has time on his hands and is known in the community as being "available to be of assistance." Alvin says, "I simply enjoy helping."

Alvin is a community painter, fix-it guy, and all-around helper. Alvin assists older people and others with sundry tasks. He drives older people to appointments, grocery shopping, and errands; for many, Alvin is their mobility. He delivers cars for those who need a driver. He drives busy people's cars to service stations for maintenance.

> These older adults *show up*; they invest their time and pay attention.

Alvin greatly enjoys and deeply respects other people. He smiles easily, is a good listener, and pays attention to people's stories. He says, "I enjoy being with people and go out of my way to be with people who some don't like." People are Alvin's passion.

Alvin often starts his day with a community coffee group that gathers to check in on one another, to talk about the weather and the news, and mostly to talk about what's going on in the community. He then goes, as he says, to "have coffee with people who are alone or who have no one or who live on the periphery of the community." He visits regularly at two senior-care homes and the area prison.

Alvin's passion for tending relationships stems in part from a powerful transformational experience in which his father held Alvin after Alvin was run over by a truck and severely injured. During these intense moments, Alvin and his father said their goodbyes, which included Alvin asking his father's forgiveness. Because of that experience, being present and honest and forgiving continue to frame Alvin's life. He says, "If you've harmed another person, there is power in going to them and saying 'I'm sorry' and asking forgiveness. Honesty and forgiveness are essential to relationships."

At eighty-one, Alvin is physically, emotionally, and spiritually healthy. Alvin believes that "God is there for us." He gives "God first credit and then my wonderful father when I was young and now my wife." Alvin lives out of gratitude. He says, "My life is truly blessed, most particularly through my family and my community."

Frank and Joan: Generative Companionship

The power of generative presence is evident in a different but equally meaningful manner in Frank's and Joan's lives. Joan had a stroke at age forty-nine and could no longer teach. After a year and a half of rehabilitation, during which she was mostly confined to a wheelchair, she became a classroom mentor and soon a long-term volunteer in the children's outreach ministry at her church. Frank, her husband, retired at age fifty-seven from upper-level leadership in manufacturing.

Joan's stroke has significantly shaped Frank and Joan's last twenty-five years. Frank has been Joan's primary caregiver, and she has been his entrée into expansive leadership roles in their congregation. Joan, age seventy-four, and Frank, age seventy-three, are resilient individuals and a resilient, vital couple. Together they have made strong, delightful contributions to each other and their community. They credit "our faith . . . our Christian beliefs; our education . . . we are well-educated and curious; our upbringing . . . we were raised to be tough; our spirit and character . . . we are both 'ornery'; and our significant financial and medical resources."

Frank and Joan enjoy traveling, though it requires careful planning so that Joan can keep her balance and get around in a wheelchair. Frank drives Joan daily to the outreach program at church that develops the learning capacity of children. The program has been a major win-win for Joan. Her presence has made significant contributions to the lives of many kids. In response, the children revere and honor her. A young Hispanic woman in the program, whose family refers to Joan as *the Teacher*, returned as an adult to say thanks and celebrate Joan's presence in her life and Joan's influence on the young woman's career as an educator. Later, Joan was invited to the young woman's wedding.

Because Frank drives Joan to choir practice, she encouraged him to stay and join the choir. Frank got involved and became a major support for the choir's ministry. As a result of Joan's encouragement, Frank's volunteering has expanded throughout the congregation; presently, he is on the church council.

Frank is an exemplary caregiver and care receiver; so is Joan.

Generative Presence: Its Forms and Contexts

Alvin, in his helpful availability, has become a unifying and generative force in his community. Frank and Joan have become a generative presence in their congregation and in each other's lives. This generative presence of Frank, Joan, and Alvin—this being there, being with, being available for—is also evident in the lives of most of the elders I met across the country. This capacity to be present was in large part because they were mostly free from earning a living, keeping a schedule, and chasing the demands of full-time commitments. These elders were not unlike many of the elders of the Old Testament, who were freed from the hard labor of making a living in an agricultural society and were able to reflect on their life experiences and be available to accompany, teach, and mentor the next generation.

The generative presence evidenced in these elders' lives took three distinct forms among the elders interviewed:

- Presence with Oneself—A result of having more time and freedom for personal reflection
- Presence as Accompanier—To be available to family, friends, and community
- Presence as a Constructive Contributor—While participating with family, friends, and community

Presence with Oneself

Among these elders, the freedom that came with retirement and older adulthood, while both bane and blessing, created opportunities for them to live differently. There was freedom from the pressures and expectations of always producing. It was as though a "load was lifted" and they were "traveling lighter." Their minds were less cluttered; their spirits less encumbered. There was freedom to be and become. They express this freedom in many ways. One says, "These are relaxed, good days. I don't need to do more. I am now a be-er more than a doer. I enjoy sitting and watching the grass grow." Another reflects, "I celebrate the good days; I rest and don't do much of anything on the bad days. I don't beat myself up when I don't have energy." An elder whose energy ebbs and flows puts it this way: "So sometimes I get things done, sometimes not, I'm easy going now." These elders experience freedom from being heavily scheduled. They have open hours, even open days, to be used as they choose or in which they can just *be*. They speak of "the dramatic shift from being very busy to having time free." And being "comfortable being retired and doing little." Some even speak of "having too much free time on their hands."

A great many of the elders utilized "traveling more lightly with an abundance of time" to refocus, to reflect, to read, to do yoga, to become more introspective, to journal, and to spend time with themselves. Jesse has "developed a quiet and thoughtful orientation to life." So have Charlotte and Larry; retirement has provided them more time to pursue their ongoing questions, to reflect, to read, to better get to know themselves and each other. Phyllis has devotions in the morning and then walks and "visits her thoughts." Dale simply enjoys spending time alone.

Within the fast-paced changes in the age wave, many of the elders interviewed expressed an interesting, quiet shift running counter to the age wave's intense pace, a shift in which elders are using the freedom of this time in their lives to become less frenetic, to become better acquainted with themselves, and to become more at home in their own lives. One elder says, "I've come to really know me and be myself for the first time in my life."

There is an echo from the biblical narrative and grounding in the Christian tradition for this being still and paying attention to the depth and breadth of God's Spirit and wisdom in one's immediate and past experience. These elders are honoring the profundity of their own existence. They are being still and, in the stillness, getting to know God. They are thus better able to engage in *holy listening* as, like Alvin, they make themselves genuinely available to others.

Presence as Accompanier with Family

The freedom that accompanied retirement and aging also became the occasion for the majority of the elders to more fully accompany their immediate and extended families. Mostly this meant spending more time in the lives of their spouses, significant others, children, grandchildren, and extended family members. Martin sums up what so many of the interviewees are doing when he says, "I am determined to find as many ways as I can to express my love and care for my family. I want to be with them;

I want to hug them; I want to be a part of the village it takes to raise the children in our family." Bill rearranged his lifestyle to raise his own children and get to know his new wife's children in their blended family. Duane and his special female companion spend quality time with each other and are both present in each other's families.

These elders are present in their families in two ways:

- Accompaniment—Being present; communicating and showing up regularly
- Availability and Active Support—Being there to contribute when needed

Accompaniment: Being Present

Most of these elders who have children hold their families in their thoughts and often communicate with them. To these elders, spouse, significant other, and other family members are of primary value. Janelle rejoices, "This is the best time in my life; I get to spend quality time with my family, my children, and grandchildren." For Francis, "being there with my wife and my family is my highest priority." Because it's important for Frankie to be in touch, she regularly communicates electronically with all the members of her immediate family. Eric communicates with one of his grandkids

> This is the best time in my life; I get to spend quality time with my family, my children, and grandchildren.

either electronically or face-to-face every day. Sally is present at family milestones, such as baptisms, birthdays, and graduations. Ron has joined his wife in "refocusing my life on family after a demanding professional career." Jim says it succinctly: "My family's important." These people care and communicate with their families, whom they hold in their hearts, and stand ready to pitch in.

Availability and Support—Being There to Help

And pitch in they do. These elders act on their love for their families by consistently showing up in their lives *when needed*. Sarah has been instrumental in raising two generations of children. So too Mary and Dean, who were invited into their grandchildren's lives and became major caregivers as they supported their children in parenting their grandchildren. Dee is a "strong force" in her family alongside and behind the scenes as her daughter struggles with injuries. Ron drives his injured daughter to her therapy and appointments.

Among these elders, couples are particularly influential in each other's lives. As they age, whether married, remarried, dating, or being companions, these couples spend quality time with one another, give needed care to one or the other, and are instrumental in each other's wellness and happiness. Frank and Joan have mutually generative influence in each other's lives; he assists her with balance and mobility, and she has introduced him to a whole new world of purposeful leadership and serving others. Norman speaks of his wife as his closest companion with whom he starts the day with coffee. Cheryl and Ralph have a 2:00 p.m. coffee date every day. Will cares for his ailing wife and their household in the mornings and does errands and pursues his hobbies in the afternoons. Frankie was the primary caregiver to both a fiancé who died before they could marry and her husband, for whom she cared for six years until his death. Three months after the death of his wife, Duane couldn't imagine living alone, so he has developed a deep and life-giving relationship with a woman whose husband died. She was one of his deceased wife's best friends and has now become a cherished companion. Sally, at age eighty-four, is dating Ollie, age eighty-eight. They read books together, do courses together online or via electronic devices, and discuss poetry and philosophy. Sally says, "We have an intellectual and emotional bond and companionship that gives life to us both."

Presence with Friends and Community

These elders not only spend time alone or with their spouses and their families, they spend quality, constructive time with their friends and their neighbors and actively participate in their communities. Young elders and middle elders especially reported creating a web of participation and influence that reaches into the world around them. These older Americans are not shrinking from public engagement but are deeply involved on their own terms. Many of these elders are at the crossroads of activities that contribute to the common good.

These elders have interesting, lively friends; together, they significantly influence each other and contribute to their wider communities. Lara loves to be with groups that are younger than she, so she attends concerts and participates in intergenerational events where she is among people two generations her junior. Jake is a fixture at the local community center where he is a "spirited sparkplug" and a role model for other people of color. Naomi attends a grief group where members help each other heal; these grief-group participants have become close friends and often travel together. Beth has a friend that calls her every day. They "check in" on one another and "brighten each other's day." Alice attends an evening of food, movie, and conversation, hosted monthly and attended by other elders who enjoy one another and enrich each other's lives. Rose looks after her vulnerable and frail older-adult neighbors. Sally is companion to many of those in the care community where she lives. She "practices simple hospitality." Alvin's self-identity and place in the community are shaped by his availability and willingness to help. Whether young or old, accepted or not, at the senior center or at the prison, Alvin is a gracious presence and an ambassador of goodwill.

> Free from major public responsibilities and with discretionary time, these elders become more themselves

Attentively at Home with Self and Others

Free from major public responsibilities and with discretionary time, these elders become more themselves and are more vitally present in their marriages, families and, communities. They may be less formally engaged in economic and political structures, but they are not gone from the essential fabric of society. Rather, they emerge as a real, flexible, and attentive presence in essential webs of social life. They are elders rising among family, friends, and neighbors!

Exploration and Discussion

1. Presence is the capacity, opportunity, and commitment to be with and to accompany another. It's being here now! It can take three distinct forms:

   ■ Presence with Oneself—A result of having more time and freedom for personal reflection
   ■ Presence as Accompanier—To be available to family, friends, and community
   ■ Presence as a Constructive Contributor—While participating with family, friends, and community

   Does this description of *presence* make sense to you? If so, how does being with another, or with others in community, make a difference? What does it communicate?

2. One of the elders said: "I am determined to find as many ways as I can to express my love and care for my family. I want to be with them; I want to hug them; I want to be a part of the village it takes to raise the children in our family." Does this statement express your intentions? If so, how are you doing this daily? Weekly? Yearly? Is it

working? Perhaps family presence is not always possible or even desired. What happens then? How can one still be present with or for others?

3. Try this personal presence inventory. Spend some time journaling on each question. Then talk about your responses with others.

- How much time do you spend each day alone with yourself? How does this engage you?
- With whom do you spend your time? What of this is quality time?
- Who are the five persons closest to you? Who are the five next closest persons?
- To whom does your presence make a difference?
- How might you better spend your time with yourself and others?

5

Relationships:
Better Together

Relationships are at the core of life . . . especially this time of life. . . . And these relationships take initiative, cultivation, and maintenance or else they wane, drop away.

—Charlotte, age sixty-nine

People were created to live interdependently. . . . Life is what we share with each other. In the beginning, we are taken care of; then we can care for others. Then there comes a day when we will be taken care of again.

—John, age seventy-two

Relationships are pervasively present in almost every dimension of the fifty-three elders' lives. Relationships make up their domestic lives, including their homes, marriages, remarriages, and special companions, as well as their nuclear and extended families. Relationships shape their social circles of close and casual friendships. Most of these elders had community group relationships at their bridge clubs, community centers, volunteer organizations, and congregations. A few of the elders had caregivers who were their family and friends as well as their service providers. Most elders had multiple relationships in their public sphere, including coworkers at their part-time jobs, other volunteers, or fellow committee or board members. A few had ongoing internet friendships with persons they had met on tours or through Road Scholar.

Whether these pervasive multidimensional relationships were well-developed or dysfunctional, they mattered. They provided physical, emotional, and social support. Some webs of relationships were "anchoring communities" in which elders fit in, belonged, and were safe. Other networks of relationships supplied elders contacts with the mechanics and plumbers who maintained their cars and hot-water heaters, as well as their pickleball playmates and chiropractors. Some of the elders' family, neighborhood, and church relationships were healthy and generative; some were conflicted and convoluted. In either case, as stated above, they had impact.

Paul Tang at IBM Watson Health, said in an interview with *Next Avenue*, a Twin Cities PBS production: "Loneliness kills and disables more people than smoking. Social connectedness is one of the best contributors to meaningful longevity." Chris Farrell, who interviewed Dr. Tang, came away from the conversation convinced that loneliness is a threat to the quality of life of elders.[1] One could almost postulate, "as their relationships go, so go elders."

Impactful multidimensional relationships are at work in the fifty-three elders' lives; they are especially evident in the lives of Phyllis and Duane.

Phyllis: Generative Giver and Receiver

Seventy-nine-year-old Phyllis announced her age, saying, "In my soul, I'm not this old." Phyllis is bright and compassionate; she holds a PhD and had a distinguished career in health care. She is a self-aware person who, she asserts, "comes from a long line of strong women."

Phyllis regards her congregation as a wellspring of faith and a caring community that strongly contributes to her spirit, her friendships, and her return to fullness of life.

> One could almost postulate, "as their relationships go, so go elders."

Phyllis's husband died a year and a half ago, but she is still grieving and healing. Phyllis's grieving and healing are intensified by an additional loss; Phyllis has a quadriplegic son who was injured at seventeen.

Phyllis tends her grief in part by writing notes to those from whom she received sympathy cards at the time of her husband's death. She lets these well-wishers know that she is grateful for their thoughts and prayers and that she continues to pray for them. Phyllis has formed a group of persons who pray for each other and for those whom they know and for whom they provide care. Writing the notes and participating in the prayer group have reoriented Phyllis's outlook; through them, she says, the Spirit "has drawn me through my grief."

Phyllis was physically depleted caring for her late husband and further declined after his death; she lost weight and couldn't sleep. She says, "morning devotions, walking, and meeting new people are turning me 'back to life.'"

Phyllis has developed a "life-giving relationship" with a widowed pastor she has known since they were young. They are considering marriage or some form of committed relationship, such as being in a "spiritually committed" relationship. Phyllis is sorting it out with her partner.

Duane: Family and Community Partnerships

At eighty-four, Duane's latest period of life is marked by his wife Esther's death three years ago. As Duane puts it, "The primary force in my life has been dealing with Esther's passing." Duane continues, "three months and twenty days after Esther's death, reflecting on my life, largely alone and by myself, I became aware that this was no way to live; God didn't intend for a person to live in this kind of isolation." So Duane started a new life.

Among a group of five couples with whom Duane and Esther had been good friends, several had lost spouses. Esther's good friend Laura was a widow from one of these couples. When Duane reached out to Laura, they began spending time together and soon discovered they enjoyed each other, especially their animated conversations. With obvious delight, Duane describes their deepening relationship, saying, "we have become life companions, not wanting to marry again, but we want to take up day-to-day life with each other, with our families, our communities, and others as we travel together." "We respect and love one another."

Duane says, "Others see the liveliness of our relationship. We laugh often. We have fun. Some call us the 'cute old couple' who have drinks, talk, and laugh." Duane and Laura spend time supporting each other's families, visiting with common friends, and working with leaders in their church and community. As they do, the vitality of their relationship, the dynamics of their faith, and their can-do attitude come together to make life full, fun, and meaningful.

Duane's new relationship with Laura includes being in relationship with both their families in a way that is fulfilling and has anchored his life as he grieves Esther's death and transitions out of the family business. His career as a businessman has been a major passion for Duane, who was inducted into the Business Hall of Fame, one of the most rewarding moments for him, his family, and his employees. Now Duane is enjoying the competence of his sons and grandson as they move the business into the future. Duane is delighted to be a part of a wonderful family effectively formed and launched by Esther, who, he says, "was the smartest of us all, and its carried forward in our children."

Duane is also grateful for his many community relationships. He has strong and deep civic ties and commitments. Currently, he is following in the wake of his deceased wife's long-standing interest and leadership in the Boys and Girls Clubs of America. Duane is on their board and a leader in the purchase and renovation of a huge closed-church campus as a new and greatly expanded facility for the work of the clubs.

Duane's life is informed by a strong faith. The most exciting and engaging aspect of his life is exercising that faith through his relationships with Laura, his family, and his community, especially as he expands his late wife's legacy with the Boys and Girls Clubs.

A Variety of Relationships That Sustain

Duane and Phyllis are sustained by relationships with family, friends, community leaders, and congregation members. Relationships are the heart of Phyllis's and Duane's resiliency in the face of the death of their spouses and major lifestyle changes. Their personal, familial, congregational, and civic-relational networks are representative of the sturdy and imaginative social grounding and variety of relationships present in the lives of the elders interviewed.

The variety of generative commitments and attitudes from which these sturdy and imaginative relationships arise is evident in what the elders said in the interviews. They spoke often of the role of relationships in their lives:

- "Relationships are at the core of life . . . especially this time of life."
- "People were created to live interdependently . . . we're built for relationships."

- "Relationships are an essential part of my life."
- "Touching people's lives is important and meaningful."

They spoke of how they approach these relationships:

- "It's critical to look at life through others' eyes . . . to walk in other people's shoes."
- "Relationships call for taking initiative, for cultivation and maintenance."
- "Saying 'I love you' matters."
- "A sense of humor is the key ingredient."
- "Love is the big thing."
- "I'm asking, 'How can I be "expressive love and care" for my family?'"
- "I love to be in communities with those younger and older."
- "I watch out for seniors, for anyone old who needs help."

And they spoke of with whom and where these relationships occur:

- "My extended family is the core of my day-to-day life."
- "The senior center is my extended family of focus."
- "I'm a part of the village it takes to raise children in a family."
- "I've become socially expansive, scheduling time with interesting people."
- "My church is my spiritual and social oasis."
- "In my life, I've been blessed with two wonderful wives, two great marriages."

- "My wife's a gift; she pushes me to stay active, to do more."
- "We are walking into the future together."

The sustaining relationships among the fifty-three elders take many forms that center around common groupings or types and their related activities. Here are some forms with associated characteristics:

- Couples—This includes dating, being together, marriage, and remarriage. While many of these elders are single, most are in a variety of generative relationships with a spouse or significant other.
- Families—Included here are immediate families, extended families, blended families, and surrogate families. Most of these elders are important participants in some form of family. Many elders are actively engaged in their children's and grandchildren's lives; many of these elders are cared for in significant ways by their children.
- Friendships—This may be long-standing friendships, newly formed friendships, group friendships, task friendships, or recreational companions. These friendships have a huge place in these elders' lives and range from good companionship to everyday check-ins; there is no question, elder friendships greatly increase their quality of life.
- Faith Communities—Items often listed are senior ministries, intergenerational events, study groups, work

groups, and worship. These faith communities are major spiritual and social oases in these elders' networks; they are anchoring places where these elders are known and develop a variety of sustaining and enriching friendships.

- Community Groups—These include work groups, senior centers, adult day care, and advocacy groups. There is often a positive connection between a network of relationships in purposeful task-oriented groups in their communities and elder resilience and vitality;

- Neighborhoods and Residences—Included here are those who live next door, down the hall, or in the close vicinity. The places where these elders live provide a matrix in which they develop meaningful relationships that expand their horizons and strengthen their resiliency.

- Mentorships—Here we find guiding and being guided in new experiences and skills. Elders know things that can bring them into relationships where they become teachers and/or learners.

- Caregiving and Care Receiving—This refers to those who are cared for and who care for others. Elders provide much assistance to others and receive such assistance. Caregiving and care receiving take many forms at many levels and are a crucial set of relationships in this stage of life, especially among late elders.

- Work Places—This may include both paid jobs or volunteer-related relationships. One in five elders work, but most early and middle elders volunteer in some form or another. All of these task-related settings provide significant pools of relationships for these elders.

- Internet—Also included here are email, texting, Facebook, Instagram, and other forms of electronic communication. While not all of these elders are digitally savvy, most of them stay in touch with family and friends via the internet. Digital communication is especially important to those who are less mobile; these connections are important in and of themselves and also are significant as "connective tissue" for face-to-face interactions.

Seldom did these elders experience just one type or form of relationship. These differing expressions of relationships regularly came together in each elder's life as a unique mix, as an elder's own unique social web. The extent and quality of these relational webs was among the critical determining factors in these elders' resiliency and vitality. Depending upon the elder's circumstance and contexts, these social webs came together to provide companionship and mutual caregiving, productive partnerships, and safety nets, as well as emotional and spiritual bonds.

> The extent and quality of these relational webs was among the critical determining factors in these elders' resiliency and vitality.

We saw that Phyllis's relational web includes a faith community where she participates and is cared for, well-wishers who have sent her cards and to whom she writes and for whom she prays, partners in her prayer group, and her special male friend with whom she is in a romantic relationship.

We saw that Duane's relational web includes a faith community where he participates and is cared for, a community in which he has been imbedded long-term and is known and respected, an organization with whose board and staff he is working closely, his large extended family, and his special female companion, with whom he is graciously involved socially, emotionally, and spiritually.

The Qualities of Relationships That Sustain

In analyzing the multiple forms of elders' sustaining relationships, I noticed that those relationships that are healthy and generative are marked by certain qualities. These qualities aligned in eight clusters:

- Trustworthiness—Faithfulness, being there in difficult times, following through. As in: husband is prime caregiver for wife; wife cared for husband, sister, and mother when they were dying; caregiver for mentally challenged aunt; substitute care provider for grandchildren; live close to grandchildren to be as much help as possible; and helped raise grandchildren.

- Respect—Persons young and old, robust or fragile, being treated well. As in: taught granddaughter to drive; classroom support monitor; children's outreach volunteer; visits people who others don't like (those on the margins); listens to young people, especially those who are different; became companions to isolated persons in care facilities.

- Compassion—Love in action for each other in good times and bad. As in: assisted in raising adult child and grandchild; saw a middle son through a divorce; provided grown daughters a place to live to save money and get educated.

- Openness—Willingness to look at reality, willingness to look beyond the usual to consider new possibilities and new ways of relating and acting. As in: dating provides intellectual and emotional companionship; struggling to discern whether to marry or be in a spiritually committed relationship; widower and widow develop a life-companion relationship.

- Directness—Working life's goodness and messiness by speaking forthrightly. As in: husband and wife have ongoing honest, direct communication about end of life; attended a grief group that became a "new community" of healing and friendship.

- Mutuality—Relational reciprocity, working together to enrich others' lives. As in: daughter assists her father in working out his life; daughter is travel companion to her father in his nineties; wrote a family history; attended Boy Scout Jamboree with grandson.

- Communication—Listening and speaking about the entirety of life among those who are involved and have a stake in the relationship. As in: digitally in communication with grandkids; pays attention to people's stories;

mentored young women and listened to their stories; told her story; communicates digitally or face-to-face with family members daily.

- Imagination—willingness to look creatively beyond the usual and try new ways of enriching life. As in: husband and wife deer hunt together; coffee date with spouse at 2:00 p.m. daily; coffee and conversation every morning; sense of humor bridges spouses' different personalities; husband writing stories about his wife to tend his grieving and honor her legacy.

Duane and Phyllis responded to their losses and life changes by demonstrating many of the qualities above. Their webs of relationships supported and enlivened them and those around them. Within the network of these effective relationships, Phyllis and Duane recognized, faced, and addressed their losses and life changes and now are healing and on their way to a new normal—perhaps even to higher levels of vitality. This was also true of most of the elders interviewed.

Relational Forms and Qualities: Social Wisdom

In this description of the social attitudes and actions of the fifty-three elders' relationships, we see an effective mixing of common life connections with imaginative relational innovation. This common, strong, imaginative social wisdom provides information and examples that might well inspire and enrich the relationships of other elders. Refined, expanded, and tested, these relational types and qualities could become a "developmental relational matrix" for elders wishing to expand their relational network and enhance their relational knowledge and skill. Such relational expansion, knowledge, and skill could be available through workshops provided by vital aging centers in congregations and senior community programs. Perhaps this process of learning from and reflecting on the stories of real people living their way through the massive relational changes of the age wave could be structured digitally as a learning exchange, a relational assets exchange blog in which any and all elders might learn from one another.

From among the elders interviewed emerge the rudimentary components of a framework for other elders to enrich their own relational networks and social wisdom, social wisdom that is congruent with many of the elements of elder wisdom portrayed by Old Testament leaders. Working these possibilities in congregations and community organizations will be developed in later chapters on structuring new networks of vital aging.

Exploration and Discussion

1. One of the elders asserted: "Relationships are at the core of life . . . especially this time of life . . . And these relationships take initiative, cultivation, and maintenance or else they wane, drop away." In what ways do you take initiative to sustain and enrich your existing relationships?

2. Who would be in the web of relationships that are the core social support for your life? Draw a diagram showing the names of the persons with whom you have

these relationships, label each relationships, i.e., spouse, friend, daughter, etc. and and then draw lines indicating their connections to you and if applicable to each other. Where does this web have the greatest strength? What important relationship, if any, is missing?

3. Sustaining relationships among elders takes common forms. Look again at the list of relational groups and their accompanying descriptions on pp. 106–8 above. Spend some time thinking about these relational groups and how they impact your life. If you can, rate your experience with the groups on scale of 1 to 10, with 10 being the most satisfying in each category.

Couples	1	2	3	4	5	6	7	8	9	10
Families	1	2	3	4	5	6	7	8	9	10
Friendships	1	2	3	4	5	6	7	8	9	10
Faith Communities	1	2	3	4	5	6	7	8	9	10
Community Groups	1	2	3	4	5	6	7	8	9	10
Neighborhoods and Residences	1	2	3	4	5	6	7	8	9	10
Mentorships	1	2	3	4	5	6	7	8	9	10
Caregiving and Care Receiving	1	2	3	4	5	6	7	8	9	10
Work Places	1	2	3	4	5	6	7	8	9	10
Internet	1	2	3	4	5	6	7	8	9	10

Revisit your assessment taking note of your strengths and limitations. What here is enriching your life? What is missing? Is there an area of high priority that you might work on? Where and with whom might you do this work?

4. We found eight qualities to be present in healthy and generative relationships (see p. 108–11). They are also listed below. Put a plus (+) by the qualities that you feel are strongest in your life at the present time. Put a minus (-) by any qualities you think are missing or that you wish were a much stronger part of your life. Put an arrow (>) next to any that are present in your life but could be stronger. Put a question mark (?) next to any qualities that are not clear to you.

- Trustworthiness—Faithfulness; being there in difficult times; following through
- Respect—Persons young and old, robust and fragile treated well
- Compassion—Love in action for each other in good times and bad
- Openness—Willingness to look at reality; willingness to look beyond the usual to consider new possibilities and new ways of relating and acting
- Directness—Working life's goodness and messiness by speaking forthrightly
- Mutuality—Relational reciprocity; working together to enrich each other
- Communication—Listening and speaking about the entirety of life among those who are involved and have a stake in the relationship
- Imagination—Willingness to creatively look beyond the usual and try new ways of being together

Review your assessment and reflect on how your relational strengths work together. Where are your relational-skill weaknesses? How do they get in the way in your relationships? Discuss your discoveries with a trusted friend to get a second opinion. Consider talking with a professional counselor with the goal of developing your strengths and addressing your weaknesses.

6

Passion:
Compelling Interests

Mission is our passion . . . to be out there in the world
. . . to not veg out but to reach out with hope.

—Betty, age seventy-five, and Dan, age seventy-nine

I'm a teaser. I love giving those around me a hard time.

—Tony, age seventy-two

Nothing is more valuable than being able to give back
. . . especially among your peers.

—Jake, age seventy-five

Nearly all of the elders I interviewed show passion in their
lives. The vast majority of the fifty-three elders care deeply
about their many endeavors. Their intense, broad interests show

the depth, breadth, and fire of the human spirit. What's more, these interests often drive and light up their lives. Their interests energize, enrich imagination, and inspire.

The elders' passions come from multiple and diverse sources and find many forms of expression. For some elders, the passions arise from their life of the mind. They love poetry and they thrive on new ideas, so they read and write and gather with others to explore their thoughts and compositions. For others, the passion is art and music. They paint, they take photographs, they play an instrument in a community ensemble, and they attend concerts and stage musicals. Some of the elders' passions emerge from their deep commitments, so, for example, they advocate for minorities and the aged, they travel the world on mission trips, or they clean up their neighborhoods. Some of their passions are born of curiosity to see new places, experience new cultures, and explore new ideas; they travel, trek, cruise, and take road trips. Many elders followed their passions to learn a new skill, so they took lessons, joined teams, and became apprentice boat builders, and furniture makers. Many had more time to do the things they had loved for a lifetime: now they had time to golf three times a week, spend afternoons restoring old tractors, or start a choir and direct a musical at a care community.

The elders interviewed spoke of things they were passionate about:

- Friends and Friendship—One elder said his passion is people: listening to their stories and befriending those on the periphery of the community, including people that some in the community don't like. Another said the Friend to Friend organization is her "driving passion."

- Community Projects—One created a preschool with older adults. Her legacy and great joy is developing and sustaining a preschool where more than fifty older adults support teachers and students as senior companions and mentors.

- Reading and Books—One elder said she reads broadly and often. It enriches her writing. Another reads books with the man she is dating; they have great times discussing what they are reading.

- Writing—One elder says that she writes poetry and participates in a poetry group with other poets where she and others read and discuss their poetry. Another refers to himself as a humorist; his sense of humor comes through in the parodies he writes and reads to anyone who will listen. Another said she is an introvert, so words have become her companion and feed her creativity; writing has become the hallmark of her retirement.

- Music—One elder says singing in a men's chorus lifts his spirit. Another started a choir at her senior living community; it brings the community together and enlivens the community's culture.

- Arts, Theatre, and Concerts—One elder says she attends regularly with her friends; the events and sharing them with others contribute greatly to the richness of her life.

- Leadership—One elder said that the most exciting and engaging aspect of his life just now is cheerleading a project that will greatly benefit children in his community. Another says she enjoys taking initiative to identify and motivate other talented people; she asks, "Lord, what is it you want me to do today?" Another elder is a leader in his housing association, through his service club, and at his church. His delight is to work with others to make the world a better place.

- Volunteering—One elder describes herself as a "well-defined doer" who continues a lifetime of active engagement as a "super-engaged volunteer." Even though she tires more quickly, she loves volunteering. Another was voted Volunteer of the Year; for him, volunteering is the spark of his life.

- A Circle of Prayer Singing—One elder who survived prostate cancer says the group with which he sang prayers brought him through. Now, he leads groups of people singing their prayers of thanksgiving and petitions for the world.

- Restoring Old Tractors and Playing Golf—One elder who has been "mechanically minded" all his life enjoys restoring his or others' old tractors. Restoring old tractors and golfing are big hobbies that regularly fill up his afternoon and feed his spirit.

- Driving—One elder reported that he loves to drive, so he volunteers driving cars at an auto auction.

- Farming and Soil Conservation—One elder is deeply satisfied to be passing land well-cared for to the next generation after a lifetime of producing something of value for the world.

- Travel—One travels as much as his budget can afford, because it's a great way to learn new things. Another travels with her good friend and traveling companion and loves it. A couple travels at least three times per year both domestically and inter-nationally. Another has shifted her passion for travel since the death of her hus-band from RVs to cruises and bus trips with friends. Another couple travels internationally and domes-tically and goes on an annual snowmobile trip.

> The pursuit of their passions greatly energizes them and influences other aspects of their lives and the lives of others.

- Learning and Teaching— One describes his passion as learning at his congregation and around the world; he has taught in China and Fin-land and greatly enjoys teaching in the St. John's Great Decisions program.

These elders are not only enlivened by these many passions, they intensely pursue them. The pursuit of their passions greatly energizes them and influences other aspects of their lives and the lives of others. One can see this dynamically at work in the lives of Betty, Dan, and Joy.

Betty and Dan: Ignited for Mission

Dan retired at age fifty-eight from his career as a technician at a large manufacturing company. He has been retired twenty years. Early in Dan's retirement, a church mission trip to Haiti deeply moved both Dan and his wife Betty to care for others. The trip ignited a passion for mission that would focus and energize the rest of their lives. When asked about it, Dan and Betty say nearly in unison: "Mission is our personal and shared passion." Their motto is "don't veg out, reach out with hope."

Dan, age seventy-nine, and Betty, age seventy-five, work with two mission service organizations. They have been on twelve one- to six-week mission trips: one to Russia, one to China, six to Africa, and four to Jamaica.

Dan refurbishes computers and distributes them internationally. He has supervised the electrical wiring of hospitals and schools in Haiti, Jamaica, Uganda, Angola, Tanzania, and Russia. Betty instructs women in sewing and quilting in mission communities, which often bring differing socioeconomic and religious groups of women together. Her work has been particularly impactful in Uganda.

In addition to their mission trips, Dan and Betty travel extensively; they have taken fifty-six trips over the last seventeen years. Dan asserts, "It is important to be out there in the world"

Dan has become a leader in promoting outreach at his church. He says, "it is critical to take initiative to walk across the room, make contact with another; it gets things started."

Dan and Betty's faith community is a prime force in their lives, most especially during their later years. It provides support for their faith, a relational network, and a place where they can make a difference. Betty claims, "[it] is the social and spiritual center of our lives."

Both Dan and Betty are healthy and rigorous. Theirs is a second marriage for both. Dale and Betty have a large supportive family. From their prior marriages, Betty has two children, Dan has four. Dan reflects thankfully, "We are grateful for the resources, our health, and the time to be able to serve and travel."

Joy: Friendship Facilitator

Joy is a passionate, resilient, grateful person—a marvelous woman forged out of hardship and hope. Her family escaped to Bolivia during the Holocaust in Germany and later moved to Denmark, where she grew up and met her husband in a language class. Recently, her husband battled colon cancer. Joy rejoices, "thankfully with surgery and radiation, he is cured." Joy and her husband have three children—two daughters and one son. She much appreciates their ongoing, substantive communication with her and with one another.

Speaking of her retirement, Joy asserts, "Friend to Friend is the 'driving passion' of my life these days. I've been involved with Friend to Friend for forty-two years; I've experienced its development, expansion, decline, and rebirth."

Presently, Joy, age seventy-two, is a key participant in the new development of the organization Friend to Friend America as a 501(c); she works at it sixty hours per week in her current role, learning about and expanding the organization's fundraising.

Joy speaks of her excitement and commitment to Friend to Friend by telling a story about Eddy. "Eddy lived in a crowded care facility, where he slept tucked away on a top bunk," Joy begins. "Eddy couldn't speak. I visited him regularly, brought him gifts, and took him out of the facility for rides. We developed a strong and meaningful connection. After a while, I took him with my husband and me to church, where Eddy became a fixture. People at church accepted Eddy, delighted in Eddy, deeply loved Eddy—and Eddy loved to be there. When Eddy died, there was a huge attendance at his funeral; he's missed. Friend to Friend makes a difference."

Joy was Jewish but has become a passionate Christian. She gratefully says, "my church has become my extended family, my spiritual connection with Jesus, and a source of deep and continuing friendships."

Joy and her husband have traveled back to Denmark, where she lived and where they met. They've been back to Germany, where her family came from, and to Bolivia, where her family went to escape the Holocaust. The travel has helped Joy integrate the disparate pieces of her life.

Personal and Community Empowerment

Dan and Betty's passion to learn from new cultures and make a difference in the world was ignited by a mission trip taken at the outset of Dan's retirement. Since then, this passion has taken off in many directions and filled their lives. One pathway of passion has taken them all over the world, harnessing their knowledge and skills to enrich the lives and institutions of persons and nations underdeveloped and in need. Dan has become a techy mission enthusiast, promoting such outreach at his church, recruiting more participants, and partnering with new service providers. A second pathway has fed Betty and Dan's insatiable curiosity with an expansive schedule of world travel that has filled their lives with new learning and adventure. Dan and Betty are excited and purposeful; retirement has been the best time of their lives. Beyond their own delight and satisfaction, they have made a huge contribution to the quality of life for individuals and communities in many nations while leading and expanding the capacity of their congregation to make a difference in the world.

Joy's ongoing passion feeds her capacity to work sixty hours a week laying the financial foundations for a program that will outlive her. She's been transformed and inspired by those with whom she's worked. Joy's a woman of deep and abiding commitments whose compassion and abilities have enriched and empowered her, the lives of those in her program, and people in her congregation.

Like Dan, Betty, and Joy, who are thriving in their retirements, most of these elders' lives have opened to the freedom of organizing their time and attention from within, where their passions can figure greatly in governing their new lifestyles. Following retirement, these elders made decisions regarding the direction of their lives that set the stage for their upcoming years and filled their daily schedules. Their compelling interests and their passions strongly informed their decisions and fired their will and energy.

It is delightful to see their passions at work, bringing them not only satisfaction and joy but sustained energy that has fueled their efforts to benefit their communities. It's inspiring to listen to Betty and Dan speak of their passion for mission and see their passion unfold in twelve mission trips around the world. I was touched to hear Joy tell Eddy's Friend to Friend story and how Eddy and the congregation he attended became a gift to each other. To see Joy light up as she speaks of the power of Friend to Friend is inspiring! Janelle was obviously delighted as she spoke of elders mentoring students at the preschool she has developed. To see these elders at work at the school is to watch one elder's passion at work unleashing the power of fifty or more other elders to make a difference in the learning of children.

> Their compelling interests and their passions strongly informed their decisions and fired their will and energy.

To see these elders speak of their passions with enthusiasm and delight, and to learn of the difference they are making in their communities and congregations, echoes the New Testament experiences of Anna and Simeon, who, filled with God's Spirit, were passionately seeking and delighted in discovering the ongoing presence and action of God and gave thanks to God in witness and song.

Following the passions in the lives of these elders is in deed to discover the presence of God in their lives and the incredible force of their strength, productivity, and happiness. One can see firsthand the generative impact their passion has in their families and communities. These passions are clear evidence of God's energizing presence in elders rising!

Exploration and Discussion

1. Do a "spark hunt." Affirm and discover the compelling interests and experiences that light you up and get you going. Give a bit of thought to each of the following:

   - What have I *always wanted to do* but never had time to do?
   - What did I *used to enjoy* but have drifted away from?
   - What am I *really good at* and *enjoy doing*?
   - What am I *curious about*? What is something I might try? What is something I want to learn?
   - How do I *play*?

   Revisit your reflections. Make a list of what emerged from all of these inquiries. Identify the top three. Chose at least one to pursue over the next six months.

2. Do a passion inventory. Read through the list of passions arising from the elders interviewed in this project (see pp. 118–21). On the list below, place a plus sign (+) by those passions that interest you.

   - Friends and friendship
   - Community projects
   - Reading and books
   - Volunteering
   - Driving
   - Restoring old tractors

- Writing
- Music
- Travel
- Arts, theatre, and concerts
- Leadership
- A circle of prayer singing
- Learning and teaching
- Farming and soil conservation

What other passions would you add to this list? Review and reflect on any of the passions you highlighted or wrote down. How are you currently following your passions? If you wish to do more with your particular passion, make a plan for how this can happen.

7

Purpose: Making a Difference

Big question at this point is: Am I done? Is there more to do? Yes, I can help someone.

> —Henry, age seventy-six

I get up early. I want to accomplish something each day.

> —Mark, age seventy-eight

I'm about giving back, doing something meaningful, it's my reason for being here.

> —Bjorn, age eighty-five

"Does my life matter anymore?"
"Do I make a difference?"
"Is there any reason to get out of bed in the morning?"

Whether articulating a major life struggle or expressing day-to-day boredom, most of the fifty-three elders were wondering about the purpose of their lives. They did so especially at moments of life transition and disruption, such as retirement, giving up driving, the loss of a loved one, or the onset of early cognitive impairment. What's remarkable is that they not only wrestled with these foundational questions regarding their reason for being, they consistently came up with generative responses and imaginative ways of finding meaning in their daily lives. Their stories reflect constructive responses to three interrelated issues of meaning and purpose:

- Do I as an elder person have value? (*self-worth and self-esteem matters*)
- Do I as an elder have anything to contribute to my family, to my community, to society? (*socioeconomic and cultural-productivity matters*)
- Do I as an elder have an essential place among the generations? If so, what is it? (*anthropological, existential, and spiritual matters*)

The first two of these questions regarding worth and purpose were overt, with many elders stating them directly. For example, Mark says, "I get up early. I want to accomplish something each day." And Henry asks, "Am I done? Is there more to do?

The third question regarding an essential role among the generations was often present just below the surface of the conversations. Sarah wonders "what is life beyond eighty for?"

Debra, one of the eighty-year-old elders, expressed all three of these questions when she described the intentions that shape her behavior: "What do I do for me? What do I do for others? What needs my doing?" Consider the evocative presence of elder questions of worth, meaning, and purpose in the stories of Sarah, Ben, and Francis.

> What do I do for me? What do I do for others?

Sarah: Getting it Done

At seventy-eight, Sarah is a "well-defined doer." She knows who she is, what she thinks, and is ready to act on her convictions—and does so with verve and competence. Sarah gets things done and done well.

Sarah has spent a lifetime actively engaged in the schools, church, and community where she and her family have lived. Looking back at her life, Sarah concludes, "I have been and continue to be a super-engaged volunteer." At this stage in her life, Sarah still engages and takes initiative; she leads by identifying and motivating other talented people within the organizations for which she volunteers.

Since her husband's onset of dementia and subsequent death six years ago, Sarah manages all aspects of her fiscal and legal affairs, takes care of a large home, and is involved in the lives of her three grown sons and their families. Sarah has been heavily invested in raising two generations of children—her own and her grandson, who was born three months premature. With his birth mother unable to care for him and then dying seven months after his birth, Sarah became her grandson's hands-on, surrogate mother.

While Sarah remains energetic and dynamic, she says, "I tire quickly, and recently I had a pacemaker installed. I use medication to keep my blood pressure low, which at times adds to my tiredness, so I've had to slow down a bit."

Sarah's volunteer work is shifting from longer-term, regularly scheduled work to less frequent, more occasional work. Sarah no longer teaches Sunday school but is a confirmation mentor. She needs flexibility and times of rest in her volunteering.

Sarah's faith is deep and abiding. She is embedded in her faith community, and in turn, the Christian faith is deeply embedded in her. She says, "it's in my bones, in my being." As she has grown older, her faith has become the core of her consciousness and activities. She says, "I regularly ask God: 'Lord, what do you want me to do today? Or just now?'"

Sarah sees that the importance of her life is "in the little things I can do for others to make their life better. I believe that the smallest thing I can do today is important to God and to others." She continues, "I wonder, 'What is life beyond eighty for?' I imagine it may be in these small things that I can still do for others."

Sarah is resilient, a resiliency she muses "is born perhaps of my faith's realistic hope coupled with values and energy shaped in my earliest years on the prairies of Western North Dakota." Sarah is deeply purposeful, self-aware, and well-defined. She knows who she is and believes in herself. She knows she has value. She's a leader. As an elder, she gets things done, just as she did earlier in her life. Sarah raised her children. As an older adult, she's been raising a grandson. She volunteers still, though less often and for a shorter duration. Her faith's perspective provides the foundation and frame that ground and focus her life. She continues to form the faith of the young at her church and still recruits others to join in the mission.

Ben: Thankful Volunteer

At eighty-five, Ben's been retired twenty-three years, the first thirteen of which were devoted to volunteering as an on-site carpenter for Habitat for Humanity. Now that he is, as he says, "longer in the tooth, there are no more hammers." In the last ten years, Ben has turned to fundraising for St. Matthew's House, planning their golfing event and doing phone calls.

Ben's passion for volunteering is born of, he says, "my possessing more than ample net worth and thus having the freedom to pursue whatever I wish: to pursue my commitment to give back, to do something meaningful, to take responsibility, to have a reason to be here." For Ben, life is purposeful. He says, "I'm happy to have lived this long. Two-thirds of my life I pursued income, so I'm spending a third of my life giving back." Ben describes his life philosophy as "be realistic, be hopeful, be thankful."

Ben's first wife died twelve years ago, and a year later he married a second time. He is deeply grateful for these marriages. He exclaims, "I've been blessed with two wonderful wives—great relationships, good companions, and good mothers!"

Ben reads and plays often. He belongs to a book club made up of people with differing points of view. An average golfer, Ben enjoys playing golf three days a week.

Ben's faith and church have a central role in his life. He attends a weekly Bible study that deepens his beliefs, provides an opportunity to investigate his faith and life questions, and provides Christian fellowship. He is part of the church's Stephen Ministry team, where he finds accompanying persons in need or crisis to be meaningful and a mutual sacred experience wherein two people gathered in Christ's name discover God's presence. Utilizing all his years of Bible study, Ben presently leads an advanced study of Scripture.

Although in good health, Ben says, "I'm thinking and planning for when ill health sets in; I'm wondering about where to live? I have a daughter and son in Milwaukee, so that's probably the best place to live then. It's a big question. And then there is the question of when . . . the timing."

Ben's life is a story of graciousness, of giving back, of vocation, and of taking up responsibilities that make life better for others.

Ben's presence and life story communicate a gracious thankfulness that issues forth in a deep commitment to give back. Ben is purposeful, and it's gotten a hold of him. Ben has more than ample resources, has had two great marriages, has a vital faith community, and he's healthy. Ben is fortunate, and he realizes it and is deeply grateful. His gratitude has led to twenty-three years of volunteering in the community and his congregation. Ben's life is a story of graciousness, of giving back, of vocation, and of taking up responsibilities that make life better for others.

Francis: Gracious, Competent Leader

Francis retired at sixty-two. During his career in university research, extension education, and academic administration, Francis developed into an effective leader with critical human systems skills and superb relational qualities. Others recognized these qualities in Francis, and he was invited to serve in numerous, short-term interim positions during the early years of his retirement. Francis reflects, "I was intrigued, challenged, and grateful for these opportunities to make a difference in educational systems I value, especially right after my wife died."

Since leaving the interim leadership assignments, Francis has expanded his interests and leadership in his neighborhood, community, congregation, and international mission. Francis has volunteered at a senior living center, he's been a long-term reading buddy at his local elementary school, where he recruited others to join him, and he's provided leadership at his local Kiwanis club. He's held multiple leadership roles at his church, has been the president of the housing association where he lives, and has been instrumental in developing crop-production systems on farms in Tanzania. At age eighty, Francis continues his active involvement in many of these ongoing endeavors.

Relationships are an essential part of Francis's ongoing vital, purposeful life and leadership style. In a relational web that begins with his family and neighbors, expands to his church and community, and reaches back to friendships from his years in academia, Francis is surrounded by interesting people in whom he delights and who deeply appreciate him. Francis says, "Tending these relationships is hugely important to me and immensely satisfying."

Francis deeply appreciates both his immediate and extended families. Sharing holidays and life milestones with them is a high priority and meaningful for him and his wife. He especially appreciates each of the spouses to whom he has been married over his lifetime. His first wife died at age sixty-four, soon after Francis's retirement. He married Mary, his present wife, three years later.

Health has been a periodic concern for Francis. He had surgery and radiation to treat prostate cancer when he was sixty-four. The cancer is presently in remission. Francis has just had a knee replaced at eighty. He has moderately high blood pressure managed with medication. Recently, nerve malfunction in his lower extremities affected his driving, so he uses hand controls. He says, "these hiccups have slowed me down, they have not kept me from people and service."

Francis reflects, "My life these days flows from gratitude, from thanksgiving for my solid beginnings with influential mentors, from gratitude for my family with all their care, and from heartfelt thanks for all the opportunities that have resulted in financial security and an incredibly interesting and rich life." It is evident that Francis's gracious, purposeful life flows from this wellspring of gratitude.

Francis has had and continues to live a purposeful life. He knows himself and relates well to others; he enjoys his humanity and the humanity he sees in others. He's a leader who see his calling to serve others, to live his life so that his family, his community, his congregation, his world might thrive. He works with a great variety of people to improve life, whether in his family, the neighborhood, at school, or halfway around the world. As an elder, Francis leads by investing what he's learned about leadership over a lifetime. During his academic career, Francis educated university students. As an elder, he continues to educate students, albeit younger ones, and still recruits others to join him. Francis spent a career in academic research and development, assisting farmers getting water in timely manner to their crops; now he's helping Tanzanian farmers improve their agricultural systems.

Elderhood's Impact: Expansive Generators of Life

Do Sarah, Ben, and Francis have a reason to get out of bed and start their day? Do they contribute to the larger common good? Do they have unique and valuable roles in the cycle of life, in their intergenerational communities? From the evidence in their stories, the answer is a resounding "Yes!"

From a look at the lives of the fifty-three elders, it seems that, in part, self-worth flows from living a purposeful life. Pursuing large aims and goals is life-giving. But purpose can also be found in simple day-to-day activities. Sarah senses her value as she does the "small things that I can still do for others." Sarah's experience is corroborated by the research of Lei Yu and his fellow researchers, who found that even small goals can help motivate someone to keep going; that purpose can involve a larger goal but is not a requirement.[1] There is added benefit: gerontologists are finding that such an enhanced sense of self-worth and purpose have significant positive implications for an elder's overall health and longevity.

Elders clearly have much to contribute to their families, their communities, and society. A close look at the many contributions of the fifty-three elders interviewed gives evidence to the breadth and depth of their lives, the extent of their impact in their communities, and the significance of their roles in their worlds. One can hear it in their words that express their commitments and attitudes; one can see it in their actions and in their generative attitudes at work.

Self-worth flows from living a purposeful life

Thirty-four of the elders interviewed spoke directly about some aspect of their purposefulness and about making a difference. They also emphasized discovering what may be needed through asking "the important questions, big and small alike." Here are some of the pieces of wisdom connected to being engaged in purposeful living:

- Ask the important questions, big and small alike.
  - What do I do for me?
  - What do I do for others?
  - What needs doing?
  - Do our lives have balance?

- — Are we engaged in meaningful activities, such as learning, charity, and travel?
- — Am I including exercise, writing, reading, volunteering, or rest?
- — Am I done? Or is there more for me to do?
- — How am I being a quiet, reflective, intentional, wise person?
- — What is life beyond eighty for?
- — Lord, what do you want me to do today?
- — Where is God in my life?

- Give back as an act of thanksgiving.
  - — I'm grateful. I moved from simple beginnings to a secure life; my life is framed by thanksgiving; this is a time for giving back!
  - — I'm about giving back.

- Develop a positive attitude.
  - — Become a realistic optimist; practice realistic hope.
  - — Do little things that make life better.
  - — Look at life through others' eyes.
  - — Be happy with what you have.
  - — Celebrate the good days.
  - — It's about mindfulness.

- Faith matters. Get involved; live your faith.
  - — Church is our prime channel for serving others.
  - — Faith and spirituality are central; filter life through the eyes of faith.
  - — Spirituality: it's less about getting it right; its more about community.

- — My faith community and my faith are in my bones.
- — Church and faith are at the center of our lives.
- Take good counsel.
  - — See challenges as opportunities.
  - — Be a calculated risk-taker.
  - — Exercise the power of one.
  - — Location matters; be intentional about where you live.
  - — Love is the big thing.
  - — Take responsibility.

One can see the sense of purpose and wisdom in these elders' questions and statements. This purpose and wisdom emerge from their reflections on their lives' activities. However, these elders not only *spoke* about purposefulness and making a difference; fifty-two of the fifty-three identified an activity in their life that contributed something of value to others. Here is a list of what they are doing:

> One can see the sense of purpose and wisdom in these elders' questions and statements.

- Contributing to Families—Paying for daughter's education; housing children as they get started in their careers; managing finances for the good of the family; making spouse and family the highest priority; expressing love to family directly; being part of the village it takes to raise a family; realistically reworking their will to fit the family's needs; working through husband's death;

moving forward deceased wife's legacy; participating in Boy Scouts with son and grandson

- Volunteering—Identifying one's passion and finding a fit; finding out what's needed and what's available and getting to work; participating in Habitat for Humanity; doing outreach to kids; helping at a center for the homeless; volunteering at a senior community center; working with Presbyterian Homes; doing international mission work in Tanzania, Russia, and Uganda; volunteering as elementary-school reading buddies; leading Kiwanis; serving on the work crew at church

- Mentoring—Mentoring children; guiding newly appointed professionals; guiding the newly retired; walking beside those who have lost a spouse; providing exercise coaching for early, middle, and late elders

- Caregiving—Caring for a spouse, parent, and other older elders.

- Community Service—Serving on boards; participating part-time in nonprofit organizations; directing a nonprofit development foundation; participating in the institutions of public life / civic organizations; helping with a major community project for Boy's and Girl's Clubs; serving as a community-association leader; chairing housing-association council; being a role model for other elders

- International Mission Work—Consulting with international colleges; helping create irrigation systems in Tanzania; going on major mission trips; refurbishing computers and distributing them internationally; sewing and quilting for mission; assisting with communication technology internationally.

- Practicing Faith—Leading and participating in substantive, pervasive, engaging faith that frames, informs, and undergirds; questioning the accuracy, validity, and substance of faith by being open and reading; exploring the intellectual and emotional levels of faith; reflecting; leading advanced Bible study; leading prayer at church and participating in a prayer chain; being a Stephen minister; leading "down-to-earth prayer"

- Writing and Storytelling—Reading and talking about books on learning to live with loss; creating mother's biography; writing a book on being an African American pastor; telling stories on video.

This is an incredible array of contributions to their families, communities, and society! Here, we see a rich portrait of the important ways these elders are sustaining and enhancing the quality of life for others through their participation in private and public life. They make a real difference. They have significant vocations.

Reviewing the list of these elders' statements of purposefulness and seeing their active contributions provides evidence of their personal and communal value. These elders are inspirational and instructional. They give evidence that elders can be exemplars and even heroic! They raise the promise of elders making major and necessary contributions to their community; elders can inspire others to join them in good, right, and beautiful work. But do elders have a unique, perhaps essential place in the human life cycle?

Elders' Responsibilities in Society

The work of these elders is evocative. It raises the question: Even as the work of these elders is unique and impactful, might it also be necessary, even essential? And if it is essential, must not elders be expected to step up and exercise their capacities and discharge the responsibilities of elderhood? Is there an essential elder societal calling? The lives of these fifty-three elders raise critical questions about an essential contribution of elders:

- Will families be able to survive the demands of work, earning a living, child-rearing, managing their domestic affairs, and addressing the disruptive challenges of illness, accident, and financial setbacks without the contributions of time, attention, and wisdom of elders?
- Will society be able to educate the young academically, socially, ethically, existentially, and spiritually without the time, attention, and wisdom of elders?
- Will society be able to care for those in late elderhood or those elders suffering from severe physical and mental impairment without the time, attention, and wisdom of early and middle elders?
- Will churches and other community organizations survive if elders don't more fully join those younger in providing wisdom, adaptive leadership, and financial resources to bridge past, present, and future?

If the answer to any or all of these questions is "yes, elders *are* essential to quality societal and church life," how might elders become effectively engaged in constructively contributing to these responsibilities? I propose that families, congregations, and communities establish generative and realistic expectations for early, middle, and late elderhood, and create the support systems for the development of strong elders and the critical exercise of their responsibilities, no matter how essential they are deemed to be. I propose that elders draw early, middle, and late elders together with children, adolescents, and emerging middle and older adults into generative conversations to explore intergenerational approaches and new ways of addressing these foundational life issues. The narratives of Scripture and the Christian tradition are instructive and can also serve as guides in these discussions. The Old Testament roles of elders in caring for the children, passing on the stories of faith, mentoring young leaders, and bridging eras of mission stand out as rich possibilities.

> Could this be the
> work of a national
> Elder Corps?

Could this be the work of a national Elder Corps? Could these tasks be raised up as a vocation, a calling for elders rising? We'll explore the possibilities in upcoming chapters.

Exploration and Discussion

1. Three important questions emerged regarding purposefulness and its place in elders' lives and their roles in

society (see p. 130 above). Reflecting on your life experience, how would you answer these questions? How would you support your answers?

- As an elder, do I have value? If so, what is it?
- As an elder, do I have anything of value to contribute to my family, my community, and society? Is so, what is it?
- As an elder, do I have an essential place in the human life cycle? If so, what is it?

2. Do a brief personal purposefulness inventory and visioning exercise. Reflect on the following:

- Who are the prime people in my life? What am I to these people?
- Toward what purpose(s) do I invest resources of thought, time, knowledge, skill, and imagination? How might I invest these resources in a way that is more in keeping with my values and my goals?
- How do I or how might I utilize what I *know* and what I can *do* to contribute to another person? To the neighborhood? To my church? To the community? To the world?
- With what persons or groups might I partner to influence or contribute to people and circumstances around me?

8

Power: Ability to Influence

I believe in the power of one.

—Eric, age eighty-two

I'm a builder. . . . My satisfaction is in moving a project from idea to completion.

—John, age seventy-two

In my research, I found that elders have significant and multiple abilities to influence people and organizations. They know how to make things happen and get things done. Much of their influence comes from their location in the web of their family, neighborhood, congregation, and community relationships. Over their lifetimes, they have come to establish friendships and working relationships with people in a great variety of economic, political, and civic enterprises. They know people in positions of power.

They belong to organizations in which they have spheres of influence. Moreover, they have experience working in the mission and activities of these organizations. John, one of the elders, asserts, regarding his work at his church, "I know how to make things happen. I go where the needs are; I work with pieces of the system. I let people know of the needs and possibilities for addressing them. Then I get people together to make decisions and get to work. Working with others is meaningful and satisfying."

> Not only do these elders have access to people and positions of influence, they possess an incredible array of knowledge and skill accumulated and refined over a lifetime.

Not only do these elders have access to people and positions of influence, they possess an incredible array of knowledge and skill accumulated and refined over a lifetime. They have owned businesses, managed companies, developed aircraft, conducted scientific experiments, built skyscrapers, run local and state governments, led churches, and written books, to just name a few of their accomplishments and capacities. This is an incredibly able bunch.

John stands out as one who is aware of his capacities and is actively harnessing his abilities to get things accomplished. In fact, most of the fifty-three elders are exercising major influence in relationships and activities in their families and their communities. These elders have impact, often significant impact, in many places in their worlds. One can see their extensive powers and expansive impact at work in Will, Norman, Ron, and Dee.

Will: Getting Things Done

Will retired a year and a half ago and moved from his farm to a small town nearby. At eighty, Will is retiring and making way for his grandson to join his son in the family farming operation. Will still helps out on their three-generation farm during planting and harvesting. Will is okay with the reversal of roles; he used to be in charge, but now his son and grandson give the orders, and he can simply enjoy the work.

Moving from the farm where she has spent most of her life is a huge adjustment for Will's wife Nora, who is ailing and needs his support and care; her sense of loss is important to Will and is a challenge addressed in his care for her.

Much goes on around Will. He says, "I'm never bored." He is the primary cook and housekeeper in their home due to his wife's illness; he spends mornings with these household tasks. When his wife sleeps in the afternoons, Will takes up his other responsibilities and his hobbies.

Because he has lived in the same area all his life and has been deeply involved in community leadership, Will has many neighbors and friends in his life, as well as new acquaintances in the housing development where he and his wife recently moved. Will serves on the area museum board and the council of his housing development. Will reflects, "I know people wherever I go . . . probably because I have lived here most of my life."

Not only has Will lived long in the community, he has been and continues to be an out-front leader. He helped bring in and continues to guide a large soybean plant, a major employer in the community. He's been on the local church council, been Sunday school superintendent, and serves on the bank board.

Will is fit and healthy. He had back surgery at forty that hasn't bothered him since. He reports, "I'm often stiff and sore in the mornings, but after a half hour on the treadmill I feel fine. The rest of the day provides more exercise, especially when I'm working on old tractors and golfing."

Will is hugely into his hobbies of restoring old tractors and playing golf. He declares, "I have been mechanically minded my entire life, beginning as a child; I enjoy restoring both my own and my neighbors' tractors." Will is also an avid golfer who plays two or three times per week with his brothers. He wistfully asserts, "I hope to play golf and restore old tractors until I'm ninety."

Will is deeply grateful for "what the good Lord has given me." His motto is: "live with what you've got." He is instrumental in passing on the farming operation to his son and grandson. In doing so, he assisted his grandson in acquiring land to get started farming. Will had a great dad, so he hopes to pass that legacy on to his son and grandson. Will believes "investing in family is the key to a strong, resilient, and happy life."

Will's faith is at the core of his values and actions. He has lived in a family with faith surrounding him, and he's been immersed in a local congregation. He sees God in the land and nature around him. He reflects, "my faith shapes how I see and feel about other people."

Norman: Family, Church, and Community Mentor

During the six years of his retirement from pastoral ministry, family has become the heart of Norman's life. He is deeply connected. His wife Liz is a close companion; they have coffee together every morning. Norman and Liz helped raise grandkids for six years. There was and still is much interaction before school and after. Norman taught his granddaughter to drive. He is among his grandchildren's most influential mentors.

Norman and Liz moved in with their children, and their children moved in with them when each was having a house built. Enhancing these deep connections in Norman's family are good boundaries, regular communication, strong support, and ample flexibility.

A local congregation and the larger church are Norman's support community and focus of activity. He volunteers at Hope Center for the homeless and leads a weekly prayer group. At age seventy-six, Norman is a mentor to newly ordained and newly retired pastors. He also mentors a "rejected young man," a kind of "prodigal son." Norman preaches periodically at a pastor friend's church. He assists with IT at the church he attends.

While Norman is mostly healthy, he says, "I swim or do exercises every other day, and I'm disciplined in what I do and eat, but I've developed heart issues that need careful tending." His wife is slowing down because of physical and mental-health issues. Norman wistfully comments, "All of this is challenging our present lifestyle of travel and the extent of our family and community involvements."

Ron and Dee: Partners in Family and Congregational Stewardship

Upon Ron's retirement, Ron and Dee relocated. With the move and with Ron's retirement came the challenge of "What to do?" Ron and Dee had moved often and had been intensely involved in ministry during Ron's career.

Dee soon discovered that she was needed to care for grandkids, to support her daughter, who was hit by a car, and to travel to tend to other members of the family. Dee began volunteering at her church and became an active participant in a women's group with whom she now has significant relationships.

As Dee sorted out all that was changing, she asked: "Where is God in my life?" At eighty-two, she has "lived into the answer." She states: "I am manager of our household, the keeper of our home." Dee is the mother of six children and continues to tend the family, supporting her children, especially during disruptions and difficult times. Dee is the matriarch—a strong, generative force in the family. Health has been a concern for Dee the past decade; she walks to exercise, but walking is now difficult because of problems with her back and balance. She is exploring new, safer ways to be active.

Ron's shift from public leadership and racial advocacy to focusing on their family has been difficult. "Down-to-earth prayer" has been important to Ron as he is making this challenging transition. Ron reflects, "Down-to-earth prayer also helps me deal with my anger, my justice 'pushiness,' that has been a major force in my life." A close friend has been a valued companion in this transition as well.

One activity of his eighty-five-year-old "rebalanced life" is driving and accompanying his daughter, who needs to get around, especially to therapy. Ron and Dee's daughter moved close to them to be supported in her healing after an accident. Ron has written a book on his role as an African American in public leadership in the church. Ron benefits from "wellness appointments," and he needs to rest more often to compensate for energy loss.

Dee and Ron have many people in their lives. Dee enjoys being with intergenerational groups of women at their church. On retreats, Dee has developed significant relationships with many women of the congregation. Dee rejoices that "the congregation has also become an important 'extended family' for our daughter, who has found a niche there for expressing her talents." Ron values the interracial, intercultural emphasis and composition of the congregation; it's a place to continue his advocacy for minorities and equality.

Ron and Dee declare, "We are walking into the future together." They regularly talk through aspects of their lives and work together on their future. They have discussed it and decided to refurbish their home so they can stay there and be cared for, should that be necessary. Ron says, "We see ourselves in this home until we die."

Ron and Dee have purchased their burial plots and planned their funerals. They are updating their will to reflect the different financial situations of their children. Spirituality and faith are central in their lives; prayer most especially for Ron, music for Dee.

Range and Force in Elder Power

Will, Norman, Dee, and Ron are powerful people who are aware of their capacities and are exercising them well. They cut a huge swath of generativity in their families and their communities. So, in varying degrees, do most of the fifty-three elders. The breadth and depth of their power is much like the capacities of Will, Norman, Dee, and Ron. Consider the varieties of power, the expansive influence, and the extensive capacities I discovered in the stories of the elders interviewed:

- Power as freedom and commitment to exercise core values
  — Freedom to choose what to do when
  — Freedom to learn and develop new skills
  — Participation in health experiments in aging
  — Capacities of discernment
  — Time and availability
  — Volunteer capacities and opportunities
  — Mentoring
  — Political clout
- Powers of competencies and capacities
  — Well-developed skills and valuable experience
  — Corporate problem solver
  — Small-repairs specialist
  — Organization developer
  — Community leader
  — Balanced strengths of proactivity, resiliency, mobility, health

- — Experienced senior conversant
- Power in financial resources
  - — Financial strength through good planning
  - — Monies for investing in projects
  - — Earning capacity
  - — Discretionary income
  - — Ample net worth; free to pursue whatever one wishes
  - — Property
  - — Reverse mortgages
- Power as trusted connections and access
  - — Community history and long-term connections
  - — Access to intersections of decision-making and grant-making
  - — Connections brought along from their workplace
  - — Power of faith in action
  - — Prayer; prayer warrior
  - — Faith and spirituality put to work

So here is evidence that as individuals, and even more so as a group or a bloc, these elders are powerful people. It's important to identify and celebrate what elders are already doing, to get the word out, to challenge the *powerless old people* myth, to chronical the work of elders over time, and to inspire others to embrace their capacity to enrich their own lives and contribute to the common good.

These elders are like elders we found earlier in the Scriptures. Their expansive and substantive capacities and influence parallel the portraits of Old Testament elders who led in their times in the history of God's chosen people. Will, Norman,

Dee, Ron, and most of the other elders interviewed exhibit the characteristics of wisdom that have emerged across the centuries among God's people. These characteristics include being centered in a firsthand relationship with God; knowing and enacting moral behavior; humbly and courageously doing the right thing in the messiness of life; interpreting present events, ideas, and actions in the light of the big picture and long view; and reflecting critically on and learning from the past, especially from mistakes, and investing these learnings in the enhancement of the present and future. We've discovered that this powerful wisdom of elders ancient and modern is most often anchored in vital faith, is lived in response to God's gifts of life and promises, and is embodied in everyday life.

> It's important to identify and celebrate what elders are already doing, to get the word out, to challenge the *powerless old people* myth

Given the patterns of our times and the strengths of a new generation of elders, I propose that groups of imaginative, assertive elders work to unleash the powers among older adults across our society. I imagine encouraging elders to join others already involved in order to harness fully the power of individual elders and elders as a generation to address the challenges of our time. This harnessing of power can serve both civic organizations and communities of faith. Imagine what could be accomplished through a national Elder Corps or through intentional integration of elder power in church settings. Its altogether possible in this new era of elders rising!

Exploration and Discussion

1. Reflect on your sphere of influence. One of the elders asserted, "I know how to make things happen. I go where the needs are; I work with pieces of the system. I let people know of the needs and possibilities for addressing them. Then I get people together to make decisions and get to work. Working with others is meaningful and satisfying." Are you a person of influence? If so, where and how are you influential? Do you know how to make certain things happen there? Do you have a sense of where the needs around you are? From your past experience, do you have access to "intersections of influence" that you might approach to address a particular need? How might you harness or activate these powers? Draw your sphere(s) of influence map.

2. Do a capacities inventory. Look at the lists of ways elders exercised power (pp. 154–55). Using those lists as a guide, respond to the following:

   ■ What are my core values, and how do I freely exercise them?

   ■ What are my competencies, and how do I exercise them?

   ■ What are my financial resources, and how do I put them to use?

- Who are my trusted connections, and where are my unique places of access? How do I exercise these?
- What are my faith resources, and how do I use them to act?

With a dialogue partner, review the capacities you have accumulated during your lifetime; then imagine and implement a plan for putting one of these capacities to work.

3. Learn a new skill and experiment practicing it. What might be new skill possibilities for you? How might you go about developing and utilizing the new skill?

4. Go to work with an organization or task force that needs your expertise in your community. What roadblocks might you encounter in trying to do this? What benefits might you gain?

9

Playfulness: Enjoyment and Leisure

Baking bread is a joy and my way of communicating love.

—Phil, age seventy

I hope to play golf and restore old tractors until I'm ninety.

—Will, age eighty

My husband and I are deer hunters; I shot a trophy buck and harvested the antlers.

—Gail, age seventy-eight

Gerontologists have long speculated but little researched what older-adult playfulness looks like and what it might contribute to an elder's quality of life. In related studies of successful aging, humor and fun consistently show up, yet little is known of what comprises this elder humor or fun and the role it plays in their lives. Careen Yarnal and Xinyi Qian capture the sense of the matter well; they write, "Few studies of adult playfulness exist; limited research on older adults and playfulness suggest that playfulness in later life improves cognitive, emotional, social and psychological functioning and healthy aging over all."[1] More importantly, in a study on the nature and influence of playfulness in older adults, they reported their discovery of twenty-three facets related to playfulness among persons over sixty-five. While much is yet to be determined about the particular role playfulness has in older adults, Yarnal and Qian's study has given us confirmation that playfulness is richly and multi-dimensionally present in elders' lives. Their twenty-three descriptors provide an interesting and inviting portrait:

▪ Happy	▪ Joyful	▪ Lighthearted
▪ Optimistic	▪ Positive	▪ Cheerful
▪ Laughs	▪ Relaxed	▪ Outgoing
▪ Fun	▪ Enthusiastic	▪ Spontaneous
▪ Carefree	▪ Open-minded	▪ Creative
▪ Whimsical	▪ Naughty	▪ Mischievous
▪ Clowning	▪ Teasing	▪ Joking
▪ Funny	▪ Humorous	

Not only does this list confirm the rich presence of playfulness in older adults, it provides glimpses of the possible connection of playfulness with the attributes that constitute quality of life: optimistic, cheerful, relaxed, enthusiastic, carefree, open-minded, creative, and whimsical. I discovered playfulness among the elders I interviewed, reflecting what Yarnal and Qian found in their study. Moreover, I found evidence of its grounding in their grace-oriented faith and the influence playfulness had in their style and quality of life.

Among the fifty-three elders, I observed much varied and impactful humor, playfulness, and time for leisure. For some elders, play and leisure are not only prevalent, they are integral to balancing their lifestyles. For others, humor is comic relief. For some, playfulness is a component of their personality, something they bring into whatever they are doing. For one elder, teasing is at the heart of his personality;

> Playfulness is richly and multi-dimensionally present in elders' lives.

Tony is affectionately known as a character in his community. For another elder, its writing humorous stories, an expression of the passion that lights up the life of one who is cognitively impaired. For others, playfulness is the way they look at life, the lens through which they view whatever they experience, whether good or bad. One can see this humor, playfulness, and leisure permeating the lives of Jolene and Jason, Sean, and Phil and Agnes.

Jolene and Jason: Diverse Senses of Humor

Jason and Jolene are eighty-four and eighty-three years old, respectively. Jason has been retired twenty years. They owned a pharmacy that now belongs to two of their four children. Jason says, "Passing on the pharmacy to our two sons has been difficult; in fact, it has been complicated and conflicted."

Jolene and Jason have lived the last five years in Judson Retirement Village. Jolene reports, "We like it a lot. We appreciate its range of enjoyable activities and its top-notch physical and social support, plus there is no maintenance work, which was one of the reasons we sold our large home."

Jolene, lively, lighthearted, and outgoing, directs a choir she started after the couple came to Judson. She's on the village leadership council. She just posed for Judson's "playboy calendar of sexy old ladies."

Jason and Jolene each have a great sense of humor. Their humor differs but is clearly a significant dimension of each of their personalities and their relationship. In fact, humor bridges their differences; Jolene is an outgoing, creative, dramatic presence, and Jason is a quiet, reflective medical professional with a wry, witty way about him.

Jason and Jolene are always dealing with loss. Jason says, "death and change are around us all the time. It's the downside of living at the retirement village." Because they live with so many older people, there are always people dying and new people arriving. Jason and Jolene's grace and sense of humor serves them well in navigating the many losses and transitions.

Jason and Jolene love to see new places, and they belong to a travel club. They have visited every area of the country and locations all over the world. Now that they are in their mid-eighties they don't travel as often; they wonder if their "traveling phase is almost over."

Both Jolene and Jason have health issues. Jason is a diabetic and has to watch his diet; he exercises regularly but lightly. Jolene has largely recovered from a bout with Lupus.

Both Jolene and Jason are persons of strong faith and a gracious spirituality. Jolene says, "the love of God keeps us going, and next to our retirement community, our church is the most important place in our life."

Jason and Jolene have a shared life motto: "Play the cards that are dealt you, because so much of life is out of your control."

Sean: Laid-Back Family Man

Sean retired in 2013 at age sixty-seven. His retirement transition was easy. Sean enjoys "sitting and watching the grass grow." During these last four years, he was the single retiree in his marriage, because his wife, Patty, who is six years younger than he, continued to work; she has now retired, so they are working out a "new life rhythm."

Sean is content. These are relaxed, leisurely days. Sean plays golf once a month. He doesn't need to play more often. He is a "be-er" rather than a doer. Sean is an introvert; he states, "I don't have . . . don't need many friends; I usually follow my wife into her friendship circles."

Both Sean and Patty's daughters are presently single and living at home with their parents. The oldest is doing so to get started in a job, pay off college debt, and save money to be able to live on her own. Their youngest daughter has returned to college to become a nurse, a profession in which she will have work. Sean worked a year longer than he had intended so that he and his wife could afford to pay for his youngest daughter's education.

Sean intends to continue to "manage his family's life well." During these early years of his retirement, Sean has completed a series of projects at his home; these projects are now mostly finished. He says his goals for his family are "financial security, significant travel for my wife and me [they own a travel trailer and travel domestically and internationally], and the launching of our daughters' careers and adult lives."

Sean grew up Roman Catholic. He left the church because they looked down on his marrying outside the faith. He became a Lutheran and says, "I enjoy a good sermon, good music, being in the community, but I have little need to be more involved."

At age seventy-one, Sean is laid-back, his basic life philosophy and immediate goal is: "Stay the course." Sean enjoys his life of leisure.

Phil and Agnes: Play and Party

Phil, age seventy, and Agnes, age sixty-six, retired when he was fifty-nine and she fifty-five. Agnes and Phil have been married twenty-two years; they have no children. Over the early years of their retirement, they have discovered that they have the freedom and financial resources to do whatever they choose.

Even though Phil grew up in a dysfunctional family, his mother treated him with a "warmth and respect" for which he is deeply grateful. Sunday school and church were important, life-giving communities for Phil and helped launch him into adulthood. For forty years, Phil has been, as he says, "a passionate, joyful bread baker." Bread is his way of communicating love and care to those important to him. Phil loves music; he finds it "is a marvelous source of inspiration, relaxation, and enjoyment." Lighthearted and open-minded, Phil loves to be in relationships and groups with those both younger and older than he.

Agnes sees this as a time for "giving back." She does Meals on Wheels and "watches out for seniors, especially anyone who needs help." She's the prime caregiver for her mother, who is ninety-six and fragile. Agnes's mother is an immigrant, which has fired Agnes's international cultural openness and global curiosity, particularly for Ireland and East Africa. Agnes says, "Meeting *others* is not only interesting, it is crucial to global understanding and peace."

Agnes and Phil report this to be "the best time in our lives. A balanced life is important and possible in early retirement." A huge component of that balance is "fun." They play tennis, bike, walk, and party; "they play and party hard." Phil says "a sense of humor is a key life ingredient." He's going for "best body of 2017." Their church is a vital contributor to Phil and Agnes's life infused with a sense of humor. They drive seventeen miles to get to their congregation's worship and its community gatherings. For Agnes and Phil, their relationships with a gracious God and within a grace-filled faith community are part and parcel of their good spirit and humor.

The Leaven of Playfulness and Leisure

Jason, Jolene, Sean, Phil, and Agnes each possess a sense of humor, play, or just hang out often. Many other elders I interviewed are also a playful lot. What does this playfulness do? What effect does leisure have in their lives?

These elders laugh, crack jokes, travel, play tennis, golf, walk, hike, canoe, sing, play instruments, restore old tractors, pose for sexy-old-ladies calendars, go for the best body of the year, read, write parodies, make videos, throw parties, host movie nights and simple conversations, rest, and relax. If old age is supposed to be a mostly sad, ever-serious, isolated existence, it most certainly is not so among these elders. There is liveliness, levity, frivolity, laughter, lightheartedness, and much just plain fun. These elders challenge the stereotype of elderhood dominated by depression and decline; they present a hopeful portrait of enjoyment in aging. More than that, they encourage and inspire all of us to more fully join "the aging party." Dale is a great model. I met, interviewed, and laughed with Dale, who is writing and reading parodies at ninety-seven and significantly cognitively impaired. Dale is a living, inspiring reminder that each of us can join that aging party on our own terms.

> These elders challenge the stereotype of elderhood dominated by depression and decline.

So what is the effect of all the humor, leisure, and playfulness? In Jason's and Jolene's lives, it enriches their relationship and assists them in dealing with their differences and the difficulties in their families. Jolene's love and enjoyment of music spread into her retirement village, drawing in other people; they sing lighthearted songs that brighten the community and heartfelt music that brings healing in the face of multiple deaths and losses. Jolene's playful posing for the sexy-old-ladies calendar sent a playful message about sex in elderhood, all the while generating laughter and self-esteem among the calendar-shoot participants and Jolene's neighbors at the senior living community.

While Sean is purposeful and well-organized, he is content to mostly just be. Older adulthood is a time for a slower pace of life for Sean. He has projects at home mostly completed. He has a few friends and that's enough. His life is well-centered in his family and his church with a little golf and travel mixed in. Sean is just plain enjoying *being*.

Phil and Agnes report that this is the "best time in our lives," enriched and enlivened by playing tennis, biking, walking, and partying hard. Their physical and emotional well-being is enhanced by having a good time. Even as Jolene at eighty-three posed for the sexy-old-ladies calendar, Phil at seventy is going for the "best body of the year." Both are sending messages that bodies and aging are good and delightful and attractive in their own way. Phil loves to bake bread; it gives him great satisfaction and becomes a bridge of love to those who receive his baking, his care, and his delight.

Domestic and international travel were the most-often cited leisure activities among these elders, especially the middle-class early and middle elders. Elders Mary and Joe are good examples. Mary, age seventy-one, and Joe, age sixty-nine, have been retired from their government jobs in Washington, DC, for twenty years. Their early retirement and adequate income has provided ample time and resources to travel

And travel they have. They moved from Washington, DC, to Florida, where they own a time share that takes them all over the world. Mary and Joe travel at least two months of the year. They have worked hospitality in Alaska three summers. They have been on countless cruises as well as trips to Europe, Russia, and Antarctica among the many, many countries and continents they have explored. Their travel and its schedules are major orienting events of their lives. For Mary and Joe, travel is exercising their curiosity, its keeping their minds active and their lives open as they learn new things.

Among the elders, travel was regularly connected to "learning new information," "expanding our horizons," "meeting new and different people," and "refreshing my hope for the world," as well as personal enjoyment. For these elders, leisure is playful, instructive, and transformative.

Sport was described as both fun and good exercise. In fact, many elders say, "the more fun the exercise, the more likely I am to keep at it." Many of these elders had experimented until they found a good combination of keeping active and play. One of the elders took up golf so he could play and expand his circle of friends. For these elders, sport is playful, but the exercise and relationship building tied to the activity are contributors to wellness.

Storytelling, video making, writing, and reading were another set of activities that ran through these elders' stories. Many of them love to read and tell stories, while some enjoy writing them or recording them. These creative activities energized and enriched the teller, the writer, the producer even as they informed, entertained, healed, and inspired their audiences. Memoirs were written, life histories were recorded, parodies were penned, and life commitments were written down and videoed. These authors revealed and better understood themselves and their lives, their audiences were better informed, and the authors and their audiences more strongly bonded. For these elders, storytelling is fun and connective; it weaves their social fabric and the past and present with the future.

Most certainly, these fifty-three elders challenge the serious, sad, tired stereotype of old age. These people are a playful lot who, in the messiness and complexity of elderhood, are light-hearted and enjoy the playfulness that enhances their lives. Playfulness seems to be a leaven that permeates theirs and others' spirits, strengthening their self-worth,

> Playfulness seems to be a leaven that permeates theirs and others' spirits

enriching their relationships, supporting physical activity, and enhancing the well-being of their communities. Playfulness enriches elders rising!

Exploration and Discussion

1. Fun, humor, leisure, enjoyment, and playfulness are plentiful among the elders of this study. Review the list of playfulness attributes on p. 160 and think back to the things that contributed to playfulness in the lives of the elders mentioned in this chapter. Then reflect on these questions:

    - How much do fun, humor, leisure, enjoyment, and playfulness exist in your life?
    - What expressions of playfulness listed in this chapter are present in your lives? What other expressions of playfulness might you add based on your life?
    - Do you have enough play? If not, how might you spend more time playing? In graceful leisure?

2. With whom do you play? Do you have enough people with whom to play? Who else might you invite to play? And how might you play together?

3. One of the elders loves to bake bread; it gives him great satisfaction and becomes a bridge of love to those who receive his bread, his care, and his delight. It seems that enjoyment and care and inspiration belong together. Think of someone whose life may need some humor, playfulness, and care. How might you play and make a difference in that person's life?

4. How do you deal with physical limitations, emotional challenges, and even financial burdens that can affect playfulness? What role does faith play in your response, if at all?

10

Peril: Vulnerability and Resiliency

I'm vulnerable. . . . I lost feeling in my feet three years ago and have to take care as I walk and drive. . . . I know that I can easily fall and injure myself . . . I see the gradual decline. . . . The key is learning to live with it.

—Sally, age eighty-four

My struggle [is] how do I be social as a single, widowed, older woman; I'm seeking to redefine "aloneness" as a friend, as a gift as well as depravation and loss.

—Sherry, age eighty-one

[I've developed] a way of life born of difficulty, grounded in faith and hope, and expressed through mindfulness, purpose, and vision.

—Bill, age sixty-eight

The perils of elderhood are extensive and impactful. The impact can be sudden, as in a loss of balance that leads to a fall and a blow to the head that causes a subdural hematoma and resulting death. Or the perils can be more complex and progressive, as in slowly losing cognitive capacities and having to discern when to stop driving, living alone, or trusting one's own judgment. Whether simple or complex, the vulnerabilities of older adulthood are real and most often progressive from one period of elderhood to the next.

The perils of elderhood are extensive and impactful.

Accurately assessing the vulnerabilities and disabilities of aging is critical to quality of life—and complicated. Often, the stereotypes of the frail old person exaggerate the amount of disability and its implications for an elder's life. A MacArthur Foundation Research report challenges this view. It states:

> Being old doesn't necessarily entail being frail. While normal human aging does involve progressively worse organ function compared to the peak of early childhood, the impact of these physiological changes on the capacity of individuals to function in society is quite modest. The exaggeration of the elderly's diminished function is due in part to archaic views that overlook the fact that people are becoming disabled later and later in their lives.[1]

If the vulnerabilities of aging are real and their onset is shifting and often overstated, accurate assessment of these matters is ever more important and difficult.

Accurately assessing and honestly addressing the vulnerabilities and perils of the aging process represent three of the most determinative factors in whether an elder thrives or languishes. Self-awareness, accurate information, and active, imaginative responses to the perils of aging are keys to this assessment process and to an elder's quality of life. The perils themselves do not determine the quality of elders' lives as much as what elders know about these perils and how elders choose to deal with them.

I found among most of the fifty-three elders interviewed a straightforward and often courageous approach to their vulnerabilities and disabilities. They demonstrated effective capacities to recognize, face, and address their perils. Consider the vulnerabilities and the coping skills at work in the lives of middle elder Betsy and late elder Carl and his wife, Debra.

Betsy: Resilient Survivor

At seventy-nine, Betsy lives year to year appreciating life's "continuity as well as facing ever new challenges and opportunities." Her most recent years have been marked by her husband's illness and his death seven years ago and, in this latest period of time, her own multiple illnesses—colon cancer, pneumonia, and uterine cancer—along with the treatments and healing involved.

She is presently undergoing chemotherapy for uterine cancer. The treatment leaves her tired and nauseated. Her last year has been particularly difficult and painful.

Betsy and her deceased husband Jason were each married before their long marriage. Jason brought five children from his former marriage into their relationship. Betsy reflects, "At first his children resented me and resisted my efforts to reach out to them. Over the years his children, their children, and their children's children have come to accept and appreciate me as mother, grandmother, and great-grandmother . . . seemingly even more after Jason's death." Because of the delicacy of the situation, Betsy has not pushed these relationships. She says, "I have rather 'just been there' and let the relationships take their course over the years." Betsy regularly prays for Jason's five children, eleven grandchildren, and six great-grandchildren.

Betsy has a robust faith that informs and undergirds every aspect of her life. Her faith deepened during the years she and her husband participated in a Bible study group with four other couples. Betsy reflects, "This group became our spiritual and social home. The members that are still alive are strong, supportive friends."

"Love is the big thing," Betsy claims. "My faith provides a working philosophy that informs every day and aspect of my life, especially these days as I face cancer, pain, and my own death." Betsy goes on, "Love is God's way of giving life; love is God's way of being in charge; . . . love never ends." Betsy's deep and ongoing understanding of the power of love is the lens through which she looks at her own life and everything around her. She says, "It anchors me; it makes me more open, more patient, more mellow."

Betsy loves to travel. She has traveled all over the world by herself and with friends. She longingly states, "I hope to heal from my cancer so a friend and I can make one more major trip."

Betsy is grateful for a friend who calls her every day. Betsy takes each day as it comes. She says: "I celebrate the good days; I rest and don't do much of anything on the bad days. I don't beat myself up when I don't have energy."

Carl and Debra: Hopeful Realists

Debra and Carl are each working with differing vulnerabilities as well as facing significant challenges as a couple. Carl, age eighty-five, and Debra, age seventy-two, met at a wilderness camp. Their relationship and marriage have been enriched by years of wilderness hiking and canoeing.

Carl grew up hiking the Sierras, and even now, though he is fragile, Carl has a small "wilderness trip in my head." More realistically, Carl and Debra are mourning the loss of their freedom to explore the wilderness either on foot or by canoe because they know, due to Carl's fragility, that their wilderness trips are over. Furthermore, they are wondering what Carl's increasing fragility will mean for their housing arrangements, medical treatment, and care.

Carl and Debra are proactive. Carl's decreasing mobility has opened for Carl and Debra an ongoing series of honest, direct conversations. They've decided it's time to talk over and do something about upcoming losses and transitions. So, they've redone their finances, they've rewritten their wills, and they've drafted health and end-of-life directives. They've both planned their funerals. Because they have no children, they are concerned about care in their older, fragile years, especially if both should not be able to care for themselves or for each other. To address these concerns, they've taken out long-term care insurance.

Carl appreciates being married to a younger woman who "pushes him" to be physically and mentally active. He speaks of Debra as "a gift." Carl has been questioning the truth and trustworthiness of his faith, so he reads, reflects, and explores. Reading author Marcus Borg has been helpful. Because spiritual openness is important to Carl, his church is particularly valuable. It is a thoughtful, reflective community where questions are welcome and explored. As Carl has tested his faith, he has decided that authentic experience is more important than logic. Carl says: "I see three levels to faith exploration: the intellect, feelings, and, in between, reflection." In his questioning, Carl has moved from conservative beginnings to becoming a Quaker and now to being a Lutheran.

Debra has many significant faith and life questions as well, and is searching for a dialogue partner with whom to explore them. While Debra experiences God and faith as real, she wonders about how they apply to her present life situation. Debra has experienced recent losses. She left her job to undertake the "difficult care for [her] dying mother." Her husband is over a decade older than she, and their life together is narrowing. Debra says, "With all these changes, I'm having to rethink myself." Meanwhile, she uses her time to "do for me, do what I do for others, and do what needs to be done."

Areas of Vulnerability

Betsy, Carl, and Debra are facing many of elderhood's vulnerabilities and perils. While navigating their own challenges in their own ways, they are representative of the pervasive sets of vulnerabilities and perils present in even larger frequency and scope among all the elders interviewed.

Interviews with the fifty-three elders identified factors that are clear indicators of vulnerability—that is, circumstances and events that cause significant risk to their quality of life. Analysis of the interviews indicates that these greatly diverse factors relate to one another to form five clusters or areas of vulnerability. Those areas are:

- Physical and cognitive decline and illnesses with accompanying caregiving challenges
- Relational losses and isolation
- Disruptive transitions
- Diminishing control of life and loss of purpose
- Financial challenges

Recognizing, Facing, and Addressing Vulnerability

While these elders face significant challenges to their quality of life, their capacities to recognize, face, and address their vulnerabilities are strengths broadly and deeply at work in their resiliency and vitality. These responsive capacities begin with recognizing—knowing, understanding, and acknowledging—the particular nature of the vulnerabilities present at any given time in their lives. As evidence of this recognition, the elders I interviewed spoke of over a hundred vulnerability factors in the five areas of their lives noted above. In many cases, the vulnerabilities and perils were present in multiples and ongoing. While most of these vulnerabilities and perils are common and well-known, reviewing a sample of them provides a glimpse of the sheer volume, breath, and depth of the challenges these fifty-three elders faced.

> **Vulnerabilities and perils were present in multiples and ongoing**

Physical and Cognitive Decline and Illnesses with Accompanying Caregiving Challenges

Along with the natural declines of aging (senescence), these elders experienced diminishing physical capacities often brought on by injuries and multiple chronic illnesses. They also experienced cognitive impairments in the form of short-term or long-term memory loss, dementia, and Alzheimer's. Here's a sampling of the physical declines and losses I discovered among the fifty-three elders I interviewed:

- Hearing loss; changes in sight; trembling hands; limited energy
- Two subdural edemas; two brain surgeries
- Lost feeling in feet
- Heart disease
- Stroke and high blood pressure
- Cancer—prostate, colon, uterine, skin, leukemia
- Diabetes
- Parkinson's disease
- Hip, knee, and shoulder replacements
- Back injuries
- Addiction, past and present
- Cognitive impairment; short-term and comprehensive memory loss

Along with the physical and cognitive decline and illness in the lives of these elders and their spouses, family, and friends, there came extensive caregiving. Vulnerabilities clustered around the challenges of tending to others, resulting at times in caregiving overload. This often led to elders asking difficult questions.

- Who will be there for me when I become frail?
- Should we invest in long-term care insurance or not?
- Do I have the capacity to care for my spouse? Will I in the future?
- How can I continue to provide help for my neighbors?
- How do I get relief from caregiving overload?

Relational Loss and Isolation

In nearly every dimension of life, these elders have experienced a variety of relational disruptions, and with these disruptions, significant emotional loss. These relational and emotional losses in some cases resulted in isolation, a major threat to elders' well-being. Here's a sample of these losses and isolation:

- Loss of wife, husband, mother, father, brother, sister, or child
- Loss of friends through death or relocation at church or in their retirement communities
- Loss of mobility, including driving or ability to travel; no more being together with
- special friends
- Loss of a friend through suicide
- Agnosticism of son; children leaving the faith
- Isolation brought on by conflict; family conflict and being cut off
- Increasingly dysfunctional marriage
- Addicted spouse

Disruptive Transitions

Elders were challenged by major shifts in place, patterns, and purpose, including transition from full-time public work, major lifestyle changes, dealing with crises, and facing relocation multiple times. These transitions were expansive and ongoing:

- Retirement from a full schedule of public work to no set schedule and private leisure
- Becoming more fragile and less mobile
- Separating from children
- Dealing with frequent residential moves that cause relocation stress syndrome; moving three times during old age: from single family home to residence with less maintenance to assisted living.
- Losing the capacity to drive; wondering when to stop driving
- No longer able to live alone; needing assistance
- Coping with a major illness
- Wondering if memory can be trusted

Diminishing Control of Life and Loss of Purpose

The major disruptions facing elders were often accompanied by diminishing life forces that presented challenges to elders' sense of personal control. Along with physical illnesses and cognitive decline came worries about inadequate medical care plans, disrupted retirement plans, crushed dreams, and life too soon narrowing—all of which undermined the elder's sense of purpose. Here's a sample:

- Life possibilities and plans narrow and the capacity to *do* is diminished
- Everyday mundane tasks become more challenging, and some become impossible

- Confusion or anxiety caused by cognitive impairment
- Threat of homelessness, feelings of helplessness regarding adequate housing
- Ongoing movement from full control to less and less control to no control
- Overwhelming forms and paperwork associated with income, medical care, and insurance
- Past life purposes disappear; possibilities for new reasons to live narrow

Financial Challenges

Major financial matters such as insufficient income, unexpected expenses, long-term care, and needing to work presented foundational life risks. Here's a sample of perils in this category:

- Too little money to sustain one's longevity
- Financial stress leading to the challenge of having to work
- Financial stress of managing one's own assets
- Sudden and unexpected financial crises
- Relationship between financial ruin and divorce
- Need for finances to support longer projected retirement
- Concern for how to pay for expensive long-term care

Just reviewing the expansive dimensions of these areas of vulnerabilities is in itself daunting. Daunting or not, these elders were courageously and constructively dealing with their vulnerabilities and perils. There was a pattern in their constructive responses that was grounded in but moved well beyond recognition. To the extent that the elders knew about their vulnerabilities, understood them, and acknowledged their presence, the elders were able to effectively face and address the vulnerabilities and limit the disabling impact on their lives. In fact, there was among most of the elders a thorough understanding of these vulnerabilities and an impressive capacity to speak directly and knowledgeably about them. They were able to accept the particular negative impacts these vulnerabilities had on their lives, put them in perspective, make an adaptive response, and get on with their lives.

> **The elders were able to effectively face and address the vulnerabilities and limit the disabling impact on their lives.**

Moreover, recognizing and facing these vulnerabilities were often accompanied by courageous decisions and concerted action that addressed the vulnerability's peril and led to less disability and more sturdy and effective living. Consider Alice.

Alice: Expansively Social

Alice, age seventy-nine, retired as a flight attendant at fifty-five. Her husband James, a fireman, retired early about the same time. For years, Alice and her husband were "wagon masters," leading RV trips across the country and on trains into Mexico.

Alice's husband died unexpectedly five years ago following back surgery. Alice continues to miss him and grieve his death, but she has also blossomed, learning to make decisions and form friendships on her own. Alice has become, as she describes herself, "more expansively social," reaching out in many directions to heal and to develop new, interesting, quality relationships.

Alice's days and weeks are structured around these events and new-found friends. Her friendships are primarily generated through two primary communities, her trailer-park neighborhood and her church. She is particularly grateful for a couple that gather a group of elders at their house for conversation, food, and a movie. The couple, Alice has noticed, also watch out for the members of the group should they need help. They watched out for her when her husband died.

Alice's extended family is small. Alice is an only child; she and her husband had one daughter. Alice's daughter lives in the Southwest and has no children. Alice enjoys her daughter and spends major holidays with her but says, "our lives are not that much connected; I do much more with my friends."

The events of 9/11 brought Alice and her husband to church. Soon after, Alice was baptized at age sixty-five. The church has become the spiritual and social center of her life. Alice is grateful that "both the people and the worship enrich my life "

Alice had a hip and a knee replaced and presently is treating a rare lung infection with antibiotics. The biggest uncertainty Alice faces regarding the future is the mystery of this infection; the doctors have been unable to either diagnose or heal it. Even as she faces her uncertain future, Alice is grateful "for my friends and faith who keep me going, and going strong."

Peril and a Pattern of Resiliency

Alice has honestly recognized the impact of her husband's death, the extent of her own physical limitations, and the realities of her struggles with an unknown and likely incurable disease. She has faced them and taken action, constructively revising her life so that she has not only survived but, as she says, "blossomed." The same is true with Betsy, whom we met earlier, who is thriving in the wake of a spouse's death, conflict with a blended family, and her own struggle with cancer and its treatment. Carl and Debra, whom we also met earlier, are also thriving, even as they wrestle with Carl's fragility, the narrowing of their life together, and their faith and life questions.

The resiliency and vitality these elders showed in the face of many perils was many times born of the optimistic realism present in Scripture and the life of faith. This optimistic realism is grounded in an honest and accurate recognition and understanding of senescence, the natural declines that come with aging. But these elders also recognized that accident, illness, and disease can be diagnosed and treated rigorously. Alice, Betsy, Carl, and Debra all adapted to the natural declines that come with aging and coupled this adaptation with an intentional and determined response to their illnesses. When this adaptation was also framed by their faith, the result was an impressive resiliency and vitality!

Most certainly and impressively, the resiliency and vitality shown in the lives of these four elders is grounded in their adaptability and courage, attitudes and behavior, faith and spirit that are present in the lives of most of the fifty-three elders. Realism and optimism, pervasive peril and determined resiliency live side by side in these elders rising!

Exploration and Discussion

1. Vulnerability, and with it risk and danger, are everywhere in elderhood. Actively recognizing, facing, and addressing these vulnerabilities and dangers are critical to an elder's quality of life. Identify and assess your vulnerabilities as best you can. Rate your level of concern or danger in each area on a scale of one to ten. Ten is the highest level of concern.

    ■ Physical Change or Decline—Diminished physical capacity; loss of hearing, sight, or balance; injury or chronic illness or disease
    1 2 3 4 5 6 7 8 9 10

    ■ Cognitive Difficulties or Decline—Short-term and long-term memory loss; dementia; Alzheimer's; senility
    1 2 3 4 5 6 7 8 9 10

    ■ Relational Disruption and Isolation—Loss of spouse, friend, or family member; family conflict and alienation; friends move away
    1 2 3 4 5 6 7 8 9 10

    ■ Critical Moment of Transition—Retiring from work; relocating living space; marital status change
    1 2 3 4 5 6 7 8 9 10

- Loss of Mobility—Can no longer drive; diminishing capability to travel; less self-reliant
  1   2   3   4   5   6   7   8   9   10
- Emotional and Spiritual Challenges—Unsettling life forces beyond my control; depression and anxiety; crushed dreams; life narrowing
  1   2   3   4   5   6   7   8   9   10
- Caregiving Concerns—Taking care of spouse, family member, or friend; helping elder neighbors; caregiver overload
  1   2   3   4   5   6   7   8   9   10
- Financial Challenges—Insufficient income; unexpected expenses; long-term care concerns; inadequate medical-care plan; needing to work
  1   2   3   4   5   6   7   8   9   10
- Spiritual Challenges—Loss of faith; questioning relationship with God; fear of the future and death; loss of faith community
  1   2   3   4   5   6   7   8   9   10
- Revisit your assessment. Are there areas of vulnerability that you are handling well? Are there areas that need further assessment and attention? How might these areas be addressed well?

2. One of the elders said: "I celebrate the good days; I rest and don't do much of anything on the bad days. I don't beat myself up when I don't have energy." What do you make of her attitude as she faces physical decline and

chronic illness? How would you describe your attitude as you face your vulnerabilities and their threats?

3. What is your history of recognizing and facing threats? Have you experienced patterns of denial and procrastination? If so, how might those patterns be interrupted and transformed? Are there patterns of accurate and timely attention and response to threat? How might you reinforce and follow those healthy ways of behaving?

4. Identify three primary supporters you would be most likely to go to for help in addressing the physical, mental, emotional, social, financial, ethical, and spiritual threats in your future? If you have not already done so, let them know you would like to turn to them for consultation and support.

5. How do spiritual practices, such as prayer, worship, meditation, or other practices fit into your handling of vulnerability and threat?

11

Living with Loss

Old age is learning to live with loss.

—Mohsin Hamid[1]

There is a sacredness in tears. They are not the mark of weakness, but of power. They speak more eloquently than ten thousand tongues.

—Washington Irving[2]

Tending my grief is always with me; it is a major concern and an ongoing task in my life. On the way, storytelling . . . [is] my pathway of healing and bridge to the future.

—Burt, age ninety-two

One of the constants in the lives of the fifty-three elders I interviewed was their experience of loss—losses of every kind. Early elders experience many losses, but the middle elders experience more, and late elders, as you would suspect, experience the most. For these elders, to live long and longer was to live with more and more loss in multiple areas of their lives.

The expansive and pervasive losses among the elders came in every dimension of their existence. Everyone experienced some type and degree of physical loss, including having less energy; diminished strength, agility, and mobility; loss of skin vitality and slower healing time; and decreased resiliency. Most of the elders had some level of hearing impairment. Many of the elders experienced some loss of cognitive capacity. Every one of the elders identified one or more significant persons in their life who had died or who became disabled. Spouses, family members, friends, work partners, conversation companions, and spiritual mentors were among the significant persons most often mentioned. Most elders had moved once or more and left behind the emotional security and meaningful memories attached to a much-loved home, a lake place, a congregation, or a region of the country. Most had transitioned from meaningful public employment that had defined them and structured their lives. Lifelong favorite recreational pursuits such as wilderness hiking, canoeing, tennis, and jogging had to be curtailed by some elders. Some had experienced a crisis that crushed their dreams. A few had lost their financial independence. A combination of physical, cognitive, and financial losses had taken away overall lifestyle independence for a few.

This litany of losses experienced by the elders I interviewed is daunting. It included the loss of some of their vitality and powers, the diminishing capacity of others around them, the loss of those they loved and needed most, the loss of financial security, and the loss of purposeful work. Some expressed losing their very reason to live. With loss such a big part of their lives, I wondered what makes it possible for them to go on? How do they endure? From where do they get their resiliency, and what does that resiliency look like?

> With loss such a big part of their lives, I wondered what makes it possible for them to go on?

Two of the elders, Darwin and Naomi, provide contrasting glimpses of the dangers inherent in living with loss, as well as one example of the character of resilience in living with its consequences.

Darwin: Losses Everywhere

Darwin, age sixty-five, lives at Safe Haven, a low-cost elder care facility for those who have little or no means. He moved to Safe Haven nine months ago after he fell and sustained a concussion, broken vertebrae, and other internal injuries; Darwin also has a progressive liver disease resulting in severe liver damage.

Darwin is divorced and has two sons who live across the country and never come to visit him. Darwin speaks of his friends, none of whom have visited him during his time at Safe Haven.

Darwin is in denial. He says he intends "to leave Safe Haven and go to live with my friends and then get back to my home."

Yet it seems that Darwin has few if any friends outside Safe Haven. His house is uninhabitable and encumbered with debt, he has no financial resources, and serious liver disease.

Smart and articulate, Darwin spent most of his working life as a salesman, a challenge and rush he now misses. He says, "I wish I had more energy like back then to get me up and get me going."

Darwin lights up when he speaks of the two most valued people in his life. He says, "Jonathan, the activities director here at Safe Haven, and Paul, the guy who comes weekly from church, are the best; they are my really good friends." As Darwin spoke of Jonathan and his church friend, it was the only time there was life in his voice and energy in the conversation. Mostly his affect was flat and the atmosphere in his room vacuous and heavy.

Naomi: Devastating Loss, Resilient Recovery

The death of Naomi's first husband when she was fifty-seven frames her past twenty years. When he died, she was devastated and felt guilty as a survivor; she was uncertain about what to do next. A grief support group at a local congregation became her new primary community, a place to heal and an environment in which to sort out her life. Naomi says gratefully, "through my participation in the group, I met eight widows and widowed people I've now known for nineteen years; one of whom has become my traveling companion."

Following through on a major goal she and her husband shared before he died became Naomi's vocation. She set about paying off their farm and getting her finances in order, which focused her life and claimed her time and attention for the next six years. Two persons in the community, a trusted banker and an effective farmer who rented her land, became partners in her challenging but successful financial mission.

As she became financially secure, she more actively participated in service groups and clubs in her community. She says. "It is something for me to look forward to, and it organizes my days." Naomi gratefully speaks of people from these organizations and her former grief group as "my most important friends who support me and enrich my life."

Seven years after the death of first husband, Naomi married again. Her second husband died recently. During their twelve years together, they enjoyed common interests, such as traveling and sharing a commitment to a life of faith and the church. She said the loss of her second husband has not been nearly as devastating as was the death of her first, mainly because of the strong support communities Naomi has surrounding her.

At seventy-eight, Naomi is an upbeat person who giggles and laughs easily and often. She says she is "grateful to be surrounded by people of faith who care about me and I about them." She knows herself and is well-defied. She reflects on her life: "My lifestyle is varied and easy going; sometimes I get something done, sometimes not. I am a strong-willed person, a contrarian; I often take opposing points of view. Of late I am particularly upset with some of my friends' opposition to gay rights."

Naomi's life and its resiliency are grounded in a lifelong faith that started at home, was nurtured at school, and has been sustained in congregations in which she has been active. She shared this faith commitment and devotion with both of her husbands. With a "thankful heart" and a wry smile, she summarizes her life "as being wonderfully blessed beyond my imagination— in spite of being married to a farmer-politician and pastor, all of whom I vowed never to marry."

The Many Faces of Loss

Darwin's life is filled with a great many losses that are going unattended. He's lost his spouse to divorce and is cut off from his children. His friends don't come to visit and don't seem to exist. His health is deteriorating, and his illnesses will likely take his life. He has neither work nor savings. He has no permanent place to live. In the face of all these losses, he is wholly unrealistic. He's in denial as his life is greatly diminished and narrowing. An official at his care facility and an outreach visitor from an area church are his only lifelines.

Naomi's life, on the other hand, shows what can happen when significant losses are honestly and directly attended. She has lost two spouses. She's faced financial insecurity. She's relocated. She's experienced the dislocation and disruption of her place in the community. In the face of these losses, she has tended the deep grief of the death of her first husband. Participating in a congregational grief group has helped her deal with her sorrow and find new supportive relationships, which now constitute a friendship network for her. Naomi has partnered with trusted, competent professionals to secure her once tenuous financial security. She has reconstructed a new lifestyle that includes tending the loss of her second husband. She has renewed her participation in her faith community's ministries. Naomi is a courageous, resilient survivor who is thriving.

Darwin and Naomi, each facing multiple losses across essential areas of their lives, are representative of the losses of the elders interviewed. A snapshot gives one a sense of the breadth and depth of their losses. Included in the list are losses of:

- Spouses
- Family harmony
- Mobility
- Income
- Faith and hope
- Property and possessions
- Good health
- Life dreams
- Personal identity
- Life purpose
- Family members (parents, siblings, relatives)
- Friends
- Support communities
- Careers and businesses
- Long-established residences
- Range of activities
- Place in the community
- Self-worth (generativity)

To review the scope of these losses and to observe the elders' survival is instructional, encouraging, and even empowering. It is instructional in the sense of "this is what could happen and how." It is instructional and encouraging to see what they are doing and to imagine, "I think in my own way; I could tend these and other losses in my life as well." It is empowering to discover their approaches to these losses and to be inspired by their courage and persistence.

Constructive Approaches to Loss

Darwin and Naomi approach their losses differently. Darwin lives in an imaginary present that isn't and a future that will not come. All the while he fails to work at that which could extend and enrich his life. Darwin's losses, his past addiction, and his inability to honestly address them have greatly diminished his life. On the other hand, Naomi is honestly and directly engaging her losses. With selected partners, she is constructively working through the consequences of her losses, and she is generating an interesting, purposeful life for herself as she moves on. Naomi is representative of the way the vast majority of these elders approach loss in their lives.

How these elders cope is also instructional and provides helpful, actionable ways to deal with loss. The elders' approaches to loss are expansive, varied, and engaging. Their approaches to loss included:

- Seeking communities of support
- Participating in grief groups
- Addressing the sadness
- Adaptability
- Being active
- Humor
- Remarrying
- Leaving a legacy
- Redesigning one's mission
- Serving others
- Proactive preparation

- Drawing on one's faith
- Prayer
- Faithful friends
- Mutually beneficial relationships
- Crying
- Compensation
- Sports (tennis, golf, walking)
- Playing
- Companionship and dating
- Appreciation of what one has
- Making a fresh start
- Drawing on one's strengths
- Developing a legacy
- Deepening one's spirituality
- Addressing faith's questions

While the elders gravitated to the approaches to loss that fit their personalities, strengths, and situations, most everyone relied on some form of support community and trusted friends as they worked through their grieving and healing. These caring relationships and communities accompanied them in their struggle, provided a listening ear, offered a variety of new relationships, and supplied perspectives and resources as they moved forward. Most often, these were made available through a local faith community in which the elder was anchored.

What's more, most of the elders regularly utilized more than one of these approaches in their healing. Naomi benefited greatly from participation in a grief group, and her partnerships with a banker and farmer provided the expertise to develop her farm.

Her faith community provided support and opportunities to reconstitute a new life.

While he was dying, Sally spoke with her husband about what it was like for him to die of Alzheimer's disease and for both of them to grieve his passing. She also participated in a relocation stress syndrome group where she could address the loss of place and relationships. She is now dating a person with whom she has many common interests, and she has a yearly cognitive assessment as one step in managing her advancing loss of memory.

Working with Loss

Patterns emerged from studying the constructive ways the elders in this survey worked through their losses. These patterns look much like the ongoing social-science discussions regarding the dynamics of grief and its healing. Many of these elders' responses to loss are similar to the observations of Elisabeth Kübler-Ross and David Kessler and others as they adapted the stages of death and dying to grieving.[3] Comparing the social scientists' description of the dynamics of grieving with the elders' responses to loss, I saw evidence of these stages:

> How these elders cope is also instructional and provides helpful, actionable ways to deal with loss.

- Shock—I didn't see this coming! I am overwhelmed! I can't go on!
- Denial—Is this really happening? How can this be?

- Bargaining—If only I could do this over again. What might I do so this will go away?
- Guilt—I knew I shouldn't have done that? Why have I survived and not her/him?
- Anger—Why me? This is not fair! How could this happen?
- Depression—Why bother? What's the point? I have no energy for this.
- Acceptance and Hope—I can do this. There is a way forward.
- Action—I'm putting one foot ahead of the other. I can do this much now. I've got an idea.
- Possible Together—They listen to me. I have partners in this. She's my new friend.

As the elders worked their way through this matrix of human responses, many of their honest, constructive encounters with loss actually strengthened their lives. Bill says that after working honestly and adaptively through the loss of his spouse, career, and parents, "a way of life [was] born of difficulty, grounded in faith and hope, and expressed through mindfulness, purpose, and vision." Jake, devastated after losing his business and income, was claimed by a senior community and congregation that needed his gifts, which led him to announce, "I'm enjoying a fresh and productive season of my life." In the midst of the disruption and duress of losing her spouse and her health, Betsy was wrapped in the support of her faith community. She exclaims, "Love is God's way of giving life. . . . It anchors me; it makes me more open, more patient, more mellow."

Sally lost her husband to Alzheimer's, a loss she faced directly and honestly through a video he and she made together. Through all of this she has "learned what it's like to die and the power of loss . . . and how it stays with the one grieving." On this journey, Sally's faith has sustained her and deepened; she says faith "is less about getting it right; it's more about the community of the church, about Jesus as a source of strength, as a forever presence around us that becomes mostly thanksgiving and doing together." And her life goes on with grace and vitality. Sally is now dating a man who lost his wife to cancer. Sally referenced a poem that he had written that was a healing force in both of their lives. The poem is another example of the direct and imaginative manner in which these elders are buoyed by their faith and using their strengths to address their losses.

Searching for Merry

Where did you go my cherished sweetheart?
I know you are waiting for me somewhere.
For sixty-three years we were never apart.
I feel your memories tugging at me.

Maybe you are waiting at our little green cottage
On the patio at Lake Osakis watching the boys
Cheerfully building their castles in the sand,
Or helping me push out the yellow pontoon.

Are you waiting on Melrose Avenue
Where our third born filled the happy house.

Or in the Browndale colonial house
Cooking up a batch of oatmeal raisin cookies.

Are you patiently tending your garden patches
On Cavell Avenue or out at Maple Plain
Waiting for me as the tomatoes ripen,
Or still patiently digging dandelions in vain.

Are you an angel waiting in the Stars
The terrifying cosmos gives not awareness
As I search for some signal from out there,
Your lithe form in a heavenly zodiac.

Are you walking with me by Wolfe Lake,
Hand in hand, avoiding an ugly reality
The surety that our days together were numbered,
Talking without words against a dawning finality.[4]

Even though losses of every kind are everywhere in their lives, the great majority of these elders are not undone or despairing. Through honest grieving, genuine healing, faith's realistic hope, and imaginative, adaptive recovery, they are going on with life, and in many instances, they are stronger and more resilient. They are elders rising from the hurt and pain of loss.

> Through honest grieving, genuine healing, faith's realistic hope, and imaginative, adaptive recovery, they are going on with life.

Exploration and Discussion

1. There are losses everywhere in an elder's life. The longer an elder lives, the greater the accumulation and pace of loss. Recognizing and facing these losses is a first step in grieving, healing, and moving forward. Review again the list of losses experienced by the elders on p. 197. How many of these losses have you experienced? As you review the list, write down the number of losses you have experienced in each category. When you add up the number of your losses, what does this feel like? Does it feel overwhelming? Heavy? Lonely? If so, with whom can you talk about your loss(es)?

2. These elders' approaches to loss are expansive, varied, and engaging. Review the responses listed on pp. 198–99. Then reflect on these approaches and resources and talk about the approaches you have turned to in order deal with losses in your life. Share your stories and experiences.

3. Resiliency is the ability to bounce back in the face of loss. How would you assess your current level of resiliency? What coping plans do you use to address losses in your life? If you need help sorting this out, what trusted person can you talk to about your losses, their impact on your life, and the ways you are responding.

12

Navigating Change

We are always dealing with change.

—Jason, age eighty-four

The key is learning to live with it.

—Sally, age eighty-four

Lord God, you have called your servants to ventures of which we cannot see the ending, by paths as yet untrodden, through perils unknown. Give us faith to go out with good courage, not knowing where we go, but only that your hand is leading us and your love supporting us.

—The Prayer of Good Courage[1]

Aging brings frequent, extensive, ongoing, and impactful change—change that may be filled with rich, new opportunities or challenging new dangers.

Physical changes in older adulthood are often pervasive and progressive. Varying manifestations of *cognitive change* may impact elders' quality of life incrementally or, as in some cases of dementia, may have quick and dramatic impact. One of the elders interviewed spoke concisely of the pervasive presence and critical importance of aging's physical and mental changes when he said, "health is the 'trump card' in old age, and it's always in play."

During elderhood, *social changes* rework primary and secondary relationships. Family roles and power may shift, and the longer an elder lives, the greater is both the possibility of isolation and the opportunity to develop new relationships. *Emotional changes* are manifold and complex, affecting an elder's relationships, moods, and spirit. Shifting *financial* factors may render life more tenuous or provide new avenues of exploration. *Beliefs and values* underlying an elder's perspectives and future horizons mature and are tested and challenged by new circumstances.

Change can affect us at any age, but because change is a frequent, impactful given for elders, it provides an especially large number of critical opportunities and challenges that call for thoughtful, adaptive responses. One of the most difficult factors in responding well to these changes is their sheer volume. In addition, the great variety of changes elders face makes them even more difficult to manage. It's one thing to discern how to creatively deal with the possibilities of a new location or a new relationship and quite another to manage the timing and pain of replacing a hip, to go on after a spouse's death, or to work though financial calamity. And most often, elders have to address change when one's energy and mental capacities are diminished.

So for elders, change is a given. And managing change is necessary to survive and, most especially, to thrive. Both this pervasive presence of change and the constructive management of change were evident in the lives of the elders I interviewed. Often, I found their responses to be thoughtful, imaginative, and effective. Consider the dynamics of change and response in the lives of Martin, Gary, and Rose.

> So for elders, change is a given. And managing change is necessary to survive and, most especially, to thrive.

Martin: Change and More Change

Martin is a seventy-six-year-old retired high-school history teacher who left teaching at age fifty-five. He winters in the South and lives in the upper Midwest the rest of the year. Martin and his wife Eleanor, an artist, have been married fifty-four years.

There have been three distinct periods to Martin's twenty-two years of retirement. In the first period, he and his wife built a dream home on a lake. In the eleven years Martin and Eleanor lived on the lake, they discovered that their children and grandchildren had such busy schedules they didn't have time to come to visit them. Martin and Eleanor became isolated and lonely, so they left the lake.

The second phase of retirement involved ten years traveling internationally and living and teaching in China. During the third and latest period, in order to be close to family, they have lived mostly in the upper-midwestern city where Martin spent most of his life. Martin says, "It's good to be at home in a culture we know and where we easily fit in." During this third phase of retirement, Martin has undergone knee and shoulder replacements.

As Martin reflects on retirement and its transitions, he thinks about the changes they've faced in their living circumstances: "In our early retirement years, we had three different domiciles and were mobile. In the next period, we had one domicile. What will it be in our later years? Will it soon be assisted living?"

Martin is deliberate and thoughtful. He asserts, "If you want to see God smile, plan ahead." As they plan, Martin and Eleanor's primary goal is "to express [our] love and care for [our] family." They want to say "I love you" as often and in as many ways as they can. They have supported their middle son through a difficult divorce. They regularly care for their grandchildren. Martin and Eleanor aim to be a part of the "village it takes to raise the children in our family." Their caregiving, however, extends beyond their children and grandchildren; Martin and Eleanor are major caregivers for a ninety-six-year-old relative who is physically strong and healthy, but mentally impaired.

Martin is passionate about learning and teaching; he has taught internationally and in a Great Decisions program. He is passionate about traveling and learning about the world firsthand. Martin reports, however, that "we have adequate but limited income, which puts restrictions on the amount of our travel." There is more. Martin is also eager to participate at his church where he can learn, make friends, and serve. Martin and Eleanor are avid gardeners. Martin recognizes that "finding time for and affording all this takes a bunch of thoughtful attention and careful planning."

As Martin thinks about his future, he says, "More and more, Eleanor and I are at the point of 'no control.' Often, we already can't do what we want to do, and change continues. Ultimately, faith is the foundation for the future; it provides a loving community, compassionate caregiving, and finally, resurrection."

During Martin's twenty-two years of retirement, change has occurred in nearly every aspect of life. Martin has faced and managed huge physical, relational, emotional changes, as well as geographical and cultural shifts. And the changes continue.

Rose and Gary: Changes and More Changes

Rose and Gary married in 2002 after each of their first spouses died. Even though they were married to other people, Rose and Gary have known each other since childhood. When they married, Gary and Rose moved to new places in the Midwest and the South, splitting each year between these two locations. In addition, Rose says, "our new marriage created a blended family of sorts, a family of children dispersed in many places around the country, which is a challenge." Family relationships are important to Rose, who says, "family relationships are central in my life and first priority with my time."

Gary's first wife, Lana, declined mentally and physically over a period of four years and died of Alzheimer's disease. Over those four years, Gary was Lana's primary caregiver. When he wore out toward the end of Lana's life, Gary reached out to others for help. Among those he asked to help was Rose. In fact, Lana and Rose had known each other for a long time and were friends. During their common care of Lana, Gary and Rose became closer friends; after Lana's death, they eventually married.

Five years ago, Gary was diagnosed with Parkinson's disease. While a shock initially, through a good care plan, regular exercise, and appropriate medication, Gary's illness is largely controlled, and he evidences few symptoms. Gary gladly asserts, "Although I have an illness that will eventually take my life, for now I've learned to live with it, and live well."

Rose, age eighty-four, is articulate and outgoing. She looks after those around her, especially her older friends and acquaintances; they call her their "good neighbor." She makes friends easily and has done so in both living locations. During this latest period of time, Rose has lost many friends and has been reaching out to make new ones. In making new friends, Rose says "my church, where I'm in a circle and a Stephen's Minister, and the community association where I serve have been prime settings in which to get close to new people."

Rose loves to read but has difficulty finding time; she laments, "I don't have enough time for everything I want to do."

Gary, eighty-four, is quiet and introverted with a sense of humor. He says, "I'm comfortable being retired and doing little other than my hobbies of leather working and playing the ukulele, which I have just taken up." His church is a "faith village" where Gary is known, is comfortable, and knows others. He also is a Stephen's Minister.

Gary and Rose are wondering where to live in the future. Gary has a brother in the Midwest. Gary isn't comfortable living in the South, where it's too hot for him. Rose likes living where its warm. They are asking, "What will be best when we are more fragile and need to be cared for?" "Loss of companionship" is also a major concern, especially for Rose. Should they live in the South or Midwest? Near friends? Near children, and if so, near which child? They are also wondering when to make the move?

Gary and Rose have faced ongoing multiple changes. Huge and complicated geographical, physical, relational, emotional, and communal shifts have been and still are at work in Gary's and Rose's resilient lives.

Addressing Change in Elderhood

If, during elderhood, change is frequent, extensive, ongoing, and impactful, effectively addressing change is critical to elders surviving and, most certainly, to their thriving during this ever-lengthening and complex period of older adulthood. One can see the resiliency and vitality in the lives of Martin, Gary, and Rose, even as they address the challenging changes accrued through thirty years of aging. What's more, their courage and hopefulness are inspiring. From their strong and imaginative responses, we can learn something about how other elders can, in turn, address their changes.

Managing Change: Four Active Dimensions

Four sets of factors appear in the way these elders approach the changes in their lives. The four sets of factors are:

1. Vision—Their capacity to see the big picture is foundational. These elders have the ability to put things in perspective and to bring together a sense of one's larger life purpose with one's view of a preferred future. Thus, these elders are wise, sturdy, and hopeful.

2. Traits—These elders possess characteristics that enable them to constructively engage change, develop constructive responses, and see those responses through to their effective conclusion. Here are examples of the traits I heard in the elders' stories:

   - Self-definition
   - Openness
   - Courage
   - Imagination
   - Humor
   - Faith
   - Authenticity
   - Honesty
   - Curiosity
   - Persistence
   - Toughness
   - Hope

3. Knowledge, skills, and resources—They utilize certain tools in problem solving or constructing a new life. They display resources needed to carry out effective responses to their conclusion. These tools and capacities include:

   - Honest reflection on life experiences and their elements of change
   - Supportive community

- Reframing challenges
- Active listening
- Adequate medical care
- Robust faith
- Adequate finances
- Accurate identification and description of changes encountered or underway
- Reliable working relationships
- Redesigning lifestyles
- Shedding/downsizing
- Competent psycho-social care
- Prayer and other faith practices
- Adaptive thinking and imagination

4. Approaches—These elders employ combinations of perspectives and capacities to engage and constructively navigate change. In some cases, their approaches appeared as one among other steps, at other times as patterns of response. This can be seen in Martin's imaginative approaches to the three phases of his retirement and Gary's care for his first wife, who had Alzheimer's. At times, these patterns even emerged as models for addressing the changes of old age. Here are some examples:

- Utilize personal strengths to cope, move on, grow from the experience
- Listen to / learn from others
- Take action / take risks

- Invite others in to assist
- Fit change into the ongoing construction of a balanced life
- Deliberate with trusted partners
- Experiment / learn from failure
- Imagine a new future

In the references and comments related to the factors above and their contribution to addressing change, two factors rise above the rest: (1) *connection with a supportive community*, and (2) *working relationships with one or more people.* Clearly, elders who were able to cope with changes on a long-term basis relied on people with whom they had close relationships. This included those who surrounded the elders and their families, providing knowledge, skills, and support. Sometimes these relationships worked directly to help manage the change, no matter its severity or number of dimensions—physical, relational, emotional, financial, or spiritual. Not only did these accompanying persons offer moral support, they also became partners in helping elders actively respond or adapt to the change and imagine a new future.

> Elders who were able to cope with changes on a long-term basis relied on people with whom they had close relationships.

In the opening chapter, we met Jake. His partners in navigating his huge changes were the senior-center community and his congregation where he volunteered. With Sally, relational support was provided by the community of care where she lived and by the man she was dating. With Tony, support came from his "lifeline," his best friend from church, and the care facility where he lived. For Martin, it was his family and friends. Gary and Rose relied on each other, their families, their church, and the communities in which they live. Among these elders, individual relationships, anchoring in a community, and life-tending partnerships are at the heart of managing change.

Many of the elders utilized more than one resource in managing change. From a review of their stories, it appears that the degree to which the elders utilized these factors and the degree to which they integrated the approaches influenced the effectiveness of their responses. For example, even as Bill was grieving the loss of his wife, he remarried and forged a new mission in non-profit grant-making and coaching. Sherry, whose career brought her to Africa where she lived in a beloved, supportive community, faced having to move upon retirement. She had to exchange one continent for another and leave behind her beloved friends to return to family, to writing, and to participation in a multicultural congregation in order to forge a new life.

In the four sets of factors at work in managing elderhood's changes, one finds patterns of effectiveness that represent resiliency factors in managing change in aging. An individual elder, a group of elders, or a center focused on elderhood could enhance resiliency and vitality in aging by strengthening one of more of these factors in elders. These resiliency factors can easily be integrated into the educational and caregiving ministries of faith communities. Much of the faith perspectives and faith-community dynamics explored earlier speak directly to the dynamics of managing change well. The promise of these factors of resiliency addressing change is intriguing. They present a framework for more research and the possibility of becoming one component of a Center for Vital and Resilient Aging in a congregation or community that is committed to joining and enhancing elders rising.

Exploration and Discussion

1. Elderhood is a period of ongoing change. Expecting, recognizing, and facing these changes are key factors in elder resiliency and vitality. The study identified seven broad categories of changes in the lives of the elders:

   - Physical—Changes in strength, health, balance, illnesses, comfort
   - Mental—Changes in short- and long-term memory; cognitive operations
   - Emotional—Changes in mood, anxiety, depression
   - Social—Changes in family, friendships, community relationships; isolation
   - Financial—Changes in income, expenses, investments
   - Existential—Changes in self-worth, attitude, meaning
   - Spiritual—Changes in belief, shame, guilt, hope

How many of these change categories are you experiencing? How are you managing the changes you've identified? What new changes taking place in your life are you discovering that you need to address? Who might be a partner in seizing opportunities to address changes you face? If you've finished this inventory and feel overwhelmed, speak with a trusted friend, pastor, or counselor about what's happening and how to respond constructively to the changes.

2. Review the four sets of factors identified in the study that are at work in the elders' approaches to change (see pp. 212–14). Using these positive factors as a guide, explore your own approaches to change and your capacity to handle change. Describe your capacity to see the big picture and have an overall vision of the challenges you face? What personal traits are your strengths? What tools (knowledge, skills, and resources) are available to you? What approaches do you or can you utilize to address change in your life? When finished with the exploration, select a trusted friend with whom to discuss the effectiveness of your approaches to change. Focus especially on strengths. If there are major changes unattended or you are overwhelmed, you might see a counselor.

13

Elders Rising

Old Age is not a defeat but a victory, not a punishment but a privilege.

—Abraham Heschel[1]

A mosaic of activities is within the reach of most older adults. More than any other age group, people over 50 have the resources (time, money, experience) to fill their lives with interesting, worthwhile, entertaining and enjoyable activities and experiences.

—Bob Ramsey[2]

The Adaptability of Elders Rising

Elders are rising. The rising of most of these elders is due, in large part, to their ability to adaptively develop their own wellness and wholeness. They are durable, visionary, and resourceful. They utilize the expanding physical and social services around them. Their beliefs shape their values and enliven their hopefulness. They rely on their faith communities as ongoing webs of trusting and life-giving relationships as well as avenues of service in their communities. They draw on their faith communities and beliefs to anchor, to receive, to heal, and to guide them.

Amid fast-paced, shifting realities, these elders are consciously and unconsciously crafting their own identities and pathways. There is a certain freedom at their age to center and mold their lives in their own way, in their own setting, and in their own time. Together with those around them, they create their own life mosaics. As individuals, and together with countless others, they are a robust cadre of older adults.

> Amid fast-paced, shifting realities, these elders are consciously and unconsciously crafting their own identities and pathways.

Ongoing Challenges and Elders Taking Action

The challenges of the age wave are daunting. The sheer volume of the age wave is overwhelming some social systems. Quality of life among the whole population of elders is uneven and often compromised. Not all elders are rising. While I found much vitality and resiliency among the fifty-three elders, there were individuals who were struggling. Some studies reveal that 10 percent of elders live in poverty, and I met several in this study. Furthermore, all the elders were facing ongoing challenges as they addressed their own vulnerabilities and lived with the expansive impact of the age wave.

Leadership and additional efforts and resources are needed to address the social, economic, and political challenges that come with the volume and diversity of older adults and their increasing longevity. Who will have the courage and imagination to rework the expectations and entitlements that threaten to break budgets and pit the development of the youngest among us against care for the oldest? Who will address the economic discrepancies among elders, discrepancies that confine many elders to poverty and isolation? From where will the new ideas and additional resources come?

Might not elders themselves take leadership and be major contributors? The elders in this study bring with them incredible knowledge and wisdom, competency and experience, imagination and adaptability, time and ideas that are available and ready to be transformed into greater action. Elders could benefit by expansively joining one another and other generations in addressing their emerging challenges.

Drawing on the wisdom gleaned from the elder interviews and the perspectives of the Christian tradition, I propose that elders' leadership be tapped and new resources be developed for promoting wellness and wholeness for all elders. I found in the elders' stories I heard wise leaders, imaginative ideas, adaptive responses, and evocative questions that hold promise for promoting such elder wellness and wholeness. The takeaway here is that elders themselves can be a rich resource for older adults who face challenges and are seeking to enrich their lives.

Elder Wellness Assets

I observed that the well-being of elders depends on how effectively eight key dimensions of their lives are purposefully developed. It seems from the elders' stories that when more of these dimensions are effectively attended, the outcome is increased resilience and vitality. So, what types of activities appear to lead to increased wellness? I propose we identify and practice these activities, these wellness assets, which can result in greater individual and community resiliency and vitality.

> I propose that elders' leadership be tapped and new resources be developed for promoting wellness and wholeness for all elders.

Below, within each of eight key dimensions of elders' lives are listed assets and strategies that can contribute to wellness. Imagine all of these assets and strategies overlapping and working together to provide a comprehensive narrative or portrait of societal elder wholeness. The wellness asset, activities and strategies listed are simply provided as I heard the interviewees describe them.

Physical Assets

The physical dimension of the elders' lives displayed a wide-ranging set of assets. When carefully tended they worked together to provide foundational elements for well-being. They resulted in more energy, better balance, increased strength, greater mobility, and overall well-being. One elder said, "I just feel and sleep better when I eat well and exercise often."

- Nutrition—Eating the right kinds of food and eating the right amounts at the right time were foundational to health. Managing the *living-to-eat syndrome*, in which older Americans overeat as they address their anxiety, boredom, or depression with food, rather than *eating to live is crical.*

- Exercise—Many of these elders incorporated their necessary, right-fit exercises into their routines. Low-impact exercises were the best. Mixing enjoyment with a workout was critical to staying with the exercise, and convenience and sociality were other keys to continuation. One elder took up golf to get regular exercise and be with friends.

- Assessment—Physical decline and chronic illness were ever-present in these elders' lives. Some paid careful attention to their changing physical conditions and carefully evaluated what exercises were helpful. This assessment was critical to avoiding injury and chronic pain. YMCA/YWCAs, fitness centers, and clinics were helpful resources in making these judgments and providing venues for workouts.

- Sleep—The elders spoke often of the value of three types of rest: sleep at night (often shortened and sometimes interrupted), daily naps (regular and necessary), and cat naps (nodding off when they felt the need). One elder said emphatically: "The quality of my day depends on my rest, and it isn't easy."

- Balance and Mobility Skills—A number of elders pointed to the importance of maintaining good balance and getting around without tripping and falling. Essential to their physical health, some of the elders spoke of balancing exercises they did daily. Many of them had treadmills in their homes so they could walk in the winter without fear of slipping on icy surfaces. Some swam several times a week.

- Medical Care and Timely Medical Procedures—Timely and responsive medical care were consistently referenced as assets in the elders' lives. Regular check-ups, early diagnosis, common and innovative treatments, and ready access to ongoing care made marked differences in their well-being. In some cases, ongoing, regular treatments meant the difference between life and death. On the downside, many of the elders spoke of the confusing, frustrating mass of insurance forms to be completed and the difficult decisions to be made on the basis of what was covered or not and whether to continue "extraordinary treatment" in the face of fatal illness.

- Appropriate Medications—Nearly every elder in the study was on one or more medications. Many spoke of the complicated processes of getting them right. All were grateful for the impact these medications had on their well-being. Some lamented the high cost of certain medications, and some wondered if they were on the right ones. Still, having access to correct medications was an important asset and a critical variable in their well-being.

- Replacements—Without being asked, many of the elders spoke appreciatively of their new knees, hips, shoulders, or heart values. These procedures, now common, clearly significantly increased the quality and length of these elders' lives. Several elders spoke of waiting too long for their procedures, and one elder counseled "getting it done when it starts hurting."

Mental Assets

Many of the elders made direct comments about their mental acuity or lack thereof. Some of them spoke of having regular cognitive assessments and of having adapted their lifestyle and activities accordingly. Many spoke of specific activities and diets undertaken to keep mentally sharp.

- Nutrition—Some of the elders used their diet to address their mental health. This included adding more fish, vegetables, and vitamins to their meals. Many limited their caffeine and alcohol consumption because of its impact on their consciousness and agitation.

- Activity—Many of the elders engaged in specific mental activities to help them maintain their cognitive acuity, including working puzzles, playing the piano, attending Road Scholar events, or taking online university classes.
- Neurological Care and Assessment—Some of these elders had regular appointments with a neurologist to assess their cognitive capacities. One elder, upon learning of her cognitive impairment, decided to have cognitive assessment yearly and made adjustments to her lifestyle. Parkinson's, dementia, and Alzheimer's were among the diseases in these elders' lives that were being treated and accommodated.

Emotional Assets

Addressing feelings in healthy ways was foundational in their resiliency and vitality. Grieving well was a key to healing after losses. Without empathy and compassion there was little capacity to connect and care for family and friends. In the absence of ways to experience joy and delight, life has little vitality. Many elders spoke of their experience with depression; each of these elders had a story of their journey of getting an accurate diagnosis and unfolding proper treatment. To a large extent, these elders were in touch with their feelings and were able to give expression to them.

> Grieving well was a key to healing after losses.

- Emotional Intelligence and Expression—Self-awareness was a clear asset. Most of the elders were broadly self-aware, including being in touch with their sorrow and grief over their multiple losses. Being in touch with their feelings enabled them to express their grief or pain honestly and accurately, which led to healing and being able to enjoy their family and friends.

- Taking Action—These elders often tended their emotional needs by participating in a grief group, gathering with others for prayer, writing notes to supporters, and meeting over coffee to care for one another. Simply being present with one another in good times and bad was a critical asset in feeling worth, being loved, and being safe. Humor and its cultivation were key assets in navigating ongoing physical and mental changes.

- Gratitude and Joy—While a full range of emotional experience and expression was important to these elders' quality of life, gratitude and its accompanying joy stood out as assets to resiliency and happiness. The ability to "count one's blessings" and "to give back" in response to all the goodness experienced across a lifetime were primary elements in these elders' contentment and hopefulness.

- Grief and Grieving—As stated above, the capacity to grieve was important to being able to let go and move on. It may be difficult to think of grieving as an asset, but it was clearly a major component of these elders' resilience. Many of the elders had developed the ability to grieve well as they made their way through one loss after another.

- Depression and Despair—Depression came from biological, social, and existential causation. No matter its origins, the assets of quality medical, psychological, and spiritual responses made the difference between living well and sinking under the weight of despair.

Social Assets

"As their relationships go, so go elders." Clearly, sturdy relationships, developed and cultivated, were key assets to these elders resilient and vital lives. Often, their relationships mattered most when they faced loss and ongoing change. A wide range of relational skills combined with emotional awareness were an essential combination of assets in the quality of these elders' lives.

- Primary Relationships with Families and Friends— Elders often mentioned depending on day-to-day relationships for basic support, affirmation, problem solving, and enjoyment. And these relationships needed ongoing attention because of the constant changes occurring in the elders' lives and in the lives of those closest to them. Sometimes their closest, primary relationships were provided by surrogates, such as visitors from congregations and neighbors.
- Secondary Relationships with Groups, Colleagues, and Communities—In addition to close primary relationships, a variety of social circles in their web of

relationships were great assets to the elders' identity, strength, and enjoyment. These included grief, prayer, and volunteer groups, as well as congregations and organizations that were their "anchoring communities." These communities often provided a pool of new friends after elders experienced the loss of closest relationships.

- Social Intelligence—Empathy, authenticity, and trust-worthiness were prime assets for elders sustaining ongoing quality relationships or developing new relationships in the wake of losses. Consistently, their quality of life was governed by the level of their social capacities. Being able to engage with others in a full spectrum of interaction was a key asset to dealing with sorrow or reflecting joy.

- Communication Range and Skills—Sustaining ongoing relationships, starting new relationships, and problem solving in a period of constant change required strong communication capacities. It was clearly an asset to be able to communicate well across a wide range of emotional and social situations. Many elders were becoming more adept at combining social media with their face-to-face communication abilities in order to be in better communication with those important to them.

Financial Assets

Shifting from full-time employment to part-time or no employment and managing one's finances were differing challenges for these elders, whose income ranged from below the poverty line (two were cared for by county welfare systems) to multimillionaires (three spoke of having more resources than they needed). Budgeting and living within their income were both foundational challenges and assets. Capacities of financial planning were essential. This meant focusing not only on revenue flow but also on potential longevity. As an elder's cognitive capacities dwindled, establishing shared or surrogate financial direction was critical. Together with physical and mental health, financial viability was cited among the most critical variables in elder happiness.

- Income—The value of accumulated resources and the capacity to earn more varied greatly and called for attention across the periods of aging. Combinations of social security, pensions, investments, salaried work, and county welfare were the primary sources of income. Most had planned well and had adequate resources, while some had been hit hard by the recession and by other unforeseen financial changes (e.g., major illness) and had to significantly alter their lifestyles. Some utilized reverse mortgages to support themselves. Not becoming a burden to one's children was a common concern.

- Budgeting—Living within a fixed income was a significant challenge for most of these elders. Many of them were greatly stressed by and needed assistance in handling these challenges. Items such as travel expenditures, changes in living situations, chronic illness, and increased insurance costs were just some of the budgeting challenges faced.

- Resource and Money Management—Most of these elders had personal property and/or investments. Managing these assets across twenty to thirty years of life was a challenge and required a unique set of capacities, regularly including a team or assistance of some kind. The competencies and trustworthiness of these resource persons were of critical concern and most often a key asset to elders' contentment and quality of life.

- Long-Term Care or Not—Among the most challenging decisions for these elders was whether or not to secure long-term care insurance. Two variables often cited in this discernment were chronic illnesses that could result in long-term needs and the availability of children to assist in providing care. Being able to look ahead and plan accordingly was a big asset.

- Dispensing and Dispersing of Wealth—Getting one's finances transferred to the next generation was a major concern. Many of these elders spoke of "leaving something to my/our kids," and some had fine-tuned their wills to respond to the particular needs of their children. Though often complicated and sometimes conflicted, this was regularly accomplished with the counsel of a combination of family members and financial experts.

Ethical Assets

These elders consistently faced new issues and decisions that called for ethical discernment and direction. In doing so, they sought to remain true to lifelong commitments during their different and disruptive older-adult times. They drew on and tested their long-standing values as they revisited their identity, life-purpose, meaning-making, emerging romantic relationships, and more. Working these moral issues well with trusted dialogue partners was a significant asset to these elders' quality of life.

- Guiding Values—New decisions often challenged or refined existing values and pushed these elders into unknown moral territory as they made decisions about issues such as where to live, how to expend resources, what lifestyle to pursue, whether to remarry or be together, how to determine the beneficiaries in a will, and how to address end-of-life decisions.

- Integrity—These elders were concerned that the last chapter of their life fit with the values and actions of their earlier lives. As they made decisions about their time, money, and new relationships, they sought to be true to what they believed and what had guided them during their lifetime. Dialogue with trusted family, friends, or a professional was an asset in these considerations.

- Truth Telling and Honesty—Facing physical and mental decline, multiple losses, and pervasive change, a few of the elders lived in denial and shrank from reality. Most of them, however, possessed keen self-awareness, open-mindedness, and a fierce commitment to "see and tell it like it is." Honestly and actively facing loss and change were assets and foundational to moving forward in their relationships and life decisions.

- Compassion and Care for the "Other"—As the physical and mental decline of their aging narrowed their focus and horizons, there was a dangerous pull toward isolation and self-centeredness among these elders. To the extent that they countered this pull with a turning outward, their lives were enriched and enhanced. Feeling empathy for and acting on that empathy were critical contributors to these elders' sense of worth and happiness.

Existential Assets

Multidimensional changes occurring in the foundations of these elders' lives, often over a twenty- to thirty-year period, disrupted their fundamental life understandings and lifestyle patterns. These changes led to asking three basic human questions: Who am I? With whom do I belong? Am I making a difference?

- Identity and Self-Worth—During their earlier adult lives, these elders mostly derived their identity and worth from their job, their attractiveness, or their physical prowess. Now retired, wrinkled, and less agile, the elders were reworking their sense of self. In this reworking of self-understanding and self-worth, their assets of internal sensibilities, beliefs, core values, and character were hugely influential. With the support of their primary communities, the elders not only redefined themselves, but they often became more genuinely the person they wanted to be.

- Belonging—Retirement, relocation, and a variety of relational losses often pushed these elders to form new primary relationships and seek anchoring communities. Faith communities and congregations were often major resources in this re-forming. Their ability to reconstitute their basic relationships was a significant asset that led to greater resiliency and happiness. Elder psychological maturity and social skills figured greatly in developing these new relationships.

- Making a Difference—Whether it was in the larger sense of life purpose or in day-to-day activities and accomplishments, doing something that contributed positively to another person's life or to the community's good was a key to these elders having a sense of meaning and quality of life. Helping others was clearly an asset to one's own thriving.

Spiritual Assets

These elders drew on the tenets of their faith and on their faith communities for life direction and relational support. Their beliefs, values, and commitments regarding what was true about their lives and most especially their futures were both indirectly and directly influenced by their faith. Their congregations were often anchoring communities within which they formed their identities, found support, and developed new relationships, especially following a loss of a family member or friend.

- Faith and Life Narrative—These elders drew meaning and direction directly and indirectly from their understandings of God and God's action. They often wove together their actions with their sense of God's presence in their lives. Strengthening their faith and expanding their understanding of Scripture were important to them. Faith was a clear asset for most.
- Sacred Space and Experience—Participation in a faith community or seeking other sacred spaces and experiences that made God real was crucial for these elders. At times, these places and experiences strengthened their faith as they faced questions regarding their beliefs and death.

> These elders drew on the tenets of their faith and on their faith communities for life direction and relational support.

- Vital Faith Practices—Worship, hymns, prayer, faith and life conversations, and Bible study were all mentioned as strengthening their faith, as it carried them through crises and provided healing in the wake of their losses. Most everyone in this particular group of elders referenced their active participation in these practices as one of the mainstays of their lives.

- Hope—Their trust in the promise of God's accompanying presence and their confidence in ongoing life with God forever was a big asset for dealing with changes, disease, loss, and decline as the end of their life was moving ever closer.

Working the Wellness Assets

Elders can find ways to integrate these physical, mental, emotional, social, financial, ethical, existential, and spiritual dimensions of being human into their lives. Among the elders in this study, such integration seems to be guided by the elders' values and imagination. Interesting patterns can be observed that reflect purposefulness and rich variety. These patterns create authentic and interesting mosaics of wellness. This mindfulness and imagination are especially evident in the wellness mosaics of early elders Charlotte and Larry and middle elder Sally.

Charlotte and Larry: Centered and Balanced Partners

Larry is a retired manufacturing executive; Charlotte is a retired high-school English teacher. Larry, age seventy, and Charlotte, age sixty-nine, delight in their "retirement freedom" and its opportunities as they thoughtfully and imaginatively weave family, friends, work, and play with the time and energy of their days. Charlotte muses, "This time of life is like being a teenager, except one has money and sex."

An insatiable curiosity is a prime dynamic driving and balancing Charlotte's and Larry's lives. Larry asserts the importance of asking, "What are the really important questions of this time of life? Am I done? Is there more to do? How might memories add perspective to senior years? What are responsibilities that come with this period of our lives? What do we do to give back, given all the goodness we've experienced?"

Larry and Charlotte are avid readers, especially biographies and history for Larry. Their reading provides perspective as they explore their questions.

As Larry and Charlotte wonder about how to balance their interests and activities in this season of their lives, Larry has discovered that "best is the enemy of better." Charlotte speaks of how "critical it is to look at life through others' eyes, to consider life by walking in other people's shoes." Together they have learned "the importance of considering realistic goals and living life accountable to achieving that which has impact."

Charlotte says, "relationships are at the core of life . . . especially this time of life. And these relationships take initiative, cultivation, and maintenance or else they wane, drop away." Larry agrees and "took up golf to regularly be with a group of guys."

Larry and Charlotte's family has taught them humility, that even though they ultimately don't have control over their lives, they can influence outcomes by responding compassionately and imaginatively. Their son was born with severe birth defects and wasn't expected to live. With their tender love and carefully crafted care, he lived to be twenty-eight. His life and death were at once gift and terribly difficult. There is more. Charlotte and Larry's daughter was severely injured in childhood; she survived but has limited capacity. She still lives with them. Their memory of the loss of their son and their ongoing care for their daughter deepen Charlotte and Larry's gratitude for the goodness of what they have together.

Larry and Charlotte filter life experiences through their mature faith. Their lives are firmly grounded and richly enhanced by their church. Larry speaks appreciatively of their congregation; he says: "our faith community is the primary wellspring in our lives: it sustains our faith; it supports our friendships; it's a major channel for serving others and engaging the community."

Out of these life experiences and reflections, Charlotte and Larry have formulated what they call their "life mottos": "Be happy with what you have, rather than unhappy about what you don't have." "Learn by failing." "Be grateful living in America, living with the world's top 1 percent of personal resources." Emerging from the pursuit of their questions and reflecting on their experience, Larry and Charlotte identify four essential elements that center and balance their lives:

- Good, meaningful, productive activities (occupation)
- Contributions of time and monies to others (charity)
- Quality life experiences and learning (discovery)
- Travel—Meeting new people, experiencing new places and cultures (expansion)

Charlotte and Larry are indeed expansive, intense, smart, wise, grateful people working a centered, balanced, enjoyable life mosaic.

Sally: Proactive Life Developer

The honesty, mindfulness, and imagination of a mosaic of wellness are evident in Sally's durable, meaningful, and pleasurable life. Sally is eighty-four. She is deeply grateful for her rich full days, days she takes an active hand in shaping despite daunting challenges.

Sally closed down her consulting work at age eighty, so she is free to develop the intellectual, social, physical, and spiritual dimensions of her own lifestyle. She says, "The arts, theatre, orchestra, and a poetry group combined with swimming and walking contribute greatly to the richness of this time in my life." Sally has season tickets to the theatre, regularly attends concerts, and is an active participant in a poetry reading group at the residential community in which she lives.

Four years ago, Sally moved from an apartment to Lakeside, an intentional senior community. Before living two years in the apartment, Sally lived in her own home for fourteen years after the death of her husband. Each of her decisions to move was carefully chosen and intentionally timed. Sally says, "I chose to leave my single-family home before I could no longer do the maintenance. I chose to move from my apartment into an independent-living residence at Lakeside to expand my social circles while I could still drive. I chose Lakeside because of its beautiful physical setting and rich culture of intellectual, social, and avocational opportunities."

Sally likes where she lives and says appreciatively, "Lakeside is a rich and always available community. I like seeing people in the hallways, at the pool, and during community meals. I especially like its large, diverse assortment of life-enriching opportunities, social activities, and delightful entertainment." Sally can choose when to be with others and when not; she can choose to be in as many or as few of the activities as suits her combination "extroverted and introverted personality." Sally has chosen to facilitate a Lakeside group discussion on end-of-life issues, questions, and directives.

During her moves, and in conversation with other persons at Lakeside, Sally became aware of her own relocation stress syndrome. She and others from her community have openly addressed and are intentionally working through this together. Everyone in the group has moved multiple times, and many in the group have moved unexpectedly and suddenly.

Limited physically due to loss of feeling in her feet, Sally is particularly careful as she walks and exercises. "I know that I can easily fall and injure myself or others. My eyesight is not as sharp in the dark, so I drive only in daylight." It is evident that Sally knows her vulnerabilities and factors these limitations into when, where, and how she moves about. She has developed a keen sense of her surroundings and laser-like concentration, focusing, as she says, on doing "one thing at a time."

Sally says she has discovered that "because aging brings gradual decline in capacity, the key is learning to live with it." So Sally is proactive in living out this motto. She has taken a driving course and carefully determines when, where, and how to drive or not. Sally has updated her health-care directives in consultation with her doctor, family, and others close to her. She has a yearly cognitive assessment, which helps her manage her own mental impairment. She says, "I've learned to do one thing at a time, take a break, and take longer." On her journey of decline, Sally has come to enjoy providing simple hospitality as well as being alone more often.

Family and community are essential to Sally. Her three children, two of their spouses, and her three grandsons and their wives, contribute greatly to her sense of belonging and being cared for. She and they have regular contact with one another, especially around family milestones, life celebrations, and holidays.

Sally is currently dating Ollie, an eighty-eight-year-old former teacher who also lives at Lakeside. Both she and Ollie have been wounded by past primary relational losses. Sally's husband died of Alzheimer's and Ollie's wife died of cancer. Sally and Ollie have been together two years, and Sally says we "have greatly enjoyed our emotional and intellectual companionship. Together, we read books, watch movies, do online and DVD courses, and discuss philosophy and poetry."

A Women in Philanthropy Group provides Sally meaningful community relationships as well as an opportunity to "give back and mentor." She muses, "I delight in listening to the stories of my peers and younger women as we learn from one another how to make our way and lead in the world."

Sally learned much from her husband's fourteen-year journey with Alzheimer's. Together, they honestly and directly faced his dying; they made a video of their life together during his decline. On the journey, she said: "I learned what it's like to die and the power of loss . . . and how it stays with the one grieving." Through all of this and more, Sally has become deeply spiritual, which she speaks of as "less about getting it right; it's more about the community of the church, about Jesus as a source of strength, as a forever presence around us that becomes mostly thanksgiving and doing together."

Sally is a vital and resilient elder actively healing and learning from her losses and anticipating and putting in place the elements that contribute to an expansive, ever-changing quality life. There is a center; it's Sally's life theme: "Learning to live with it." There is balance in the design of Sally's lifestyle: she fits multiple human dimensions into her high-quality existence. There is exercise; there is entertainment; there is learning new things; there is dating; there is spirituality. In all of this, Sally leans into the future via proactive readiness for what's coming.

A Mosaic of Wellness

Like Charlotte, Larry, and Sally, most of the elders interviewed are thoughtfully refocusing and reframing their lives as well as rearranging their mundane patterns of day-to-day schedules. Within certain physical and financial constraints, these elders made lifestyle choices guided by their own peculiar values, interests, and imaginations.

With time on their hands and possessing a wide range of resources, these elders embraced the opportunity to set their life direction and meaningfully order their relationships and activities toward wellness rather than being swept along by their worlds and the decline of aging. They centered and balanced and creatively integrated their wellness assets into their own unique life mosaic.

Individuals or groups of elders can use the eight wellness assets to reflect on what is happening in each dimension of life. Taken together, these assets can provide elders with a mosaic of wellness at any moment in their aging. Elders can use these assets to assess their functioning and to make plans to grow in each of these areas. The result would be an enrichment and integration of a mosaic of wellness, of an enhancement of their overall quality of life.

Elder Wellness and a Wellness Wheel

My observations of elder wellness assets, developed into a mosaic of wellness, are similar to the philosophy and strategies of the International Council on Active Aging (ICAA).[3] The ICAA's understanding of health for older adults moves from a focus on management of disease to prevention and proactive development. The ICAA's mission is to change society's perceptions of aging and improve the quality of life for aging baby boomers and older adults by focusing on seven dimensions of wellness (emotional, vocational, physical, spiritual, intellectual, social, and environmental).

The ICAA places these seven dimensions into a framework in which the dimensions integrate with one another and are centered and balanced. The wellness dimensions are coordinated and developed to provide health and vitality that merge from serving the wants and needs of an elder person's life. The council supports professionals through education, resources, and tools so that these practitioners can assist elders in achieving optimal quality of life.

While the ICAA's dimensions of wellness are not defined exactly as I observed among the elders interviewed, most of what is incorporated in the ICAA's wellness framework, including their suggested tools for promoting health, can enrich the development of the assets and mosaics of wellness I found among the interviewees. I see the ICAA's wellness framework and the mosaic of wellness complementing each other and providing rich resources for enhancing elders' resiliency and vitality.

Utilizing the Wellness Assets

Most elders possess the time and capacities for exercising the potential inherent in the wellness assets. I imagine congregations and community organizations supporting elders by designing their programs to support the activities that develop these assets. Families and congregations could utilize the assets in making life decisions and supporting elders. Society could find resources here for addressing the age wave's disruptive dynamics and the socioeconomic discrepancies in the older-adult population as communities promote wellness and wholeness among elders rising.

Exploration and Discussion

1. Elders clearly have assets they can draw upon or benefit from in all the key dimensions of their lives. What are the wellness assets at work for you? Review the lists above (pp. 222–36) and take notes on how you exercise them in your life. What assets may be missing in your life? Which do you want to cultivate, explore, or incorporate? Think about how you might advance your well-being by developing one or more of these assets.

2. Create a wellness mosaic and a wellness plan. If possible, address your key needs in each of the eight wellness assets. For example, in the physical dimension, you might say something like: "I need to take more frequent manageable walks," or "I want to find a partner who will engage with me in a fun form of exercise." When you have created a plan, talk with others about how you see it enhancing your life.

14

Elders Rising: Families and Churches

I strongly believe that we should create an organized Elder Corps . . . we need to hear more about what older people can do for young people, for their communities, and for one another.

—Ken Dychtwald[1]

Perhaps the most beautiful legacy that aging parents can leave their children is a personally lived lesson about facing old age and death with courage and grace.

—Eugene Bianchi[2]

Elders and Their Families

In this study, families were hugely influential in elders' lives. Some families were open and direct and in constructive relationships with their elders. Other families were dysfunctional, with unresolved conflict leaving elders distant and emotionally cut off. More often, the level of effectiveness in roles and relationships varied according to the challenging changes and situations facing elders and their families. In some situations, elders were integral participants in the ongoing daily dynamics of their family's life. In other situations, elders were physically and emotionally distant from their children and grandchildren. Some elders were in conflicted or passive-aggressive relationships with one or more of their children, and with this dysfunction came tension, hurt, and alienation.

> Family structures and dynamics greatly influenced the elders' well-being.

Whether functioning in a healthy way or largely dysfunctional, family structures and dynamics greatly influenced the elders' well-being. In this study, family constructive dynamics that contributed to elders' well-being emerged in six areas of family relationships and situations.

Elders and Family Transitions

With elderhood and its changes came shifts in identity, responsibilities, and power in relationships. A critical dynamic in the elders' health and strength was the ability to constructively work through the transitions that occur as they move from being a major family caregiver to becoming a mutual family participant to becoming someone who requires care from the family. Paying attention to these shifts and recalibrating their place in their families was a major ongoing process for all the elders. Recognizing and attending these shifts realistically and addressing them effectively contributed both to the elders' and to their families' quality of life. Authenticity, transparency, and direct communication were the crucial ingredients in navigating these shifts.

Staying Connected

Most of the elders spoke of their families in detail. Keeping up on their families mattered to them. Face to face and electronically, they were able to "stay in touch." However, engaging and participating in family life was much more complex and difficult. Elders and their families were often spread across great distances. In some cases, conflicted and changing roles and relationships made mutual, honest, and direct communication complicated. Elder knowledge and skill in managing these connections across their families were critical to elder and family well-being. Family members reaching out and affirmatively connecting with their elders made a huge contribution to those elders' sense of worth, support, and safety.

Letting Go

The shifting roles and relationships of elders in their families meant that these elders had to relinquish power and responsibilities at many stages in their lives and in the lives of their children and grandchildren. Awareness, self-worth, and relational skills were crucial in navigating these changes and contributed greatly to the well-being of the elders and to other members of their families. Especially important was the ability to recognize the ending of relationships and responsibilities and the redistributing of authority and control so that the elder and other members of the family could move on to healthy new stages in their lives.

Filling the Gaps

Many of the elders were significant players in the rearing of their grandchildren. Some of them took "childcare days" with grandchildren during the week in support of their grandchildren's busy parents. Some elders were back-up childcare when their grandchildren were sick; two of the elders became surrogate parents to their grandchildren when the elders' children were absent or unable to parent. Many of the elders supported their children by taking their grandchildren on weekends. In all of these commitments, the elders were significantly participating in their grandchildren's rearing. Some of them were purposefully and unobtrusively providing housing for their adult children as they got established financially. Other elders walked alongside their children, providing care during recovery from injury. Many of these elders unobtrusively added value to their children and their grandchildren as they "stood in the gaps."

Financial Planning

For elders, talking about their finances with families was important but complicated. These conversations and times of discernment were important because elders and their families were often either currently, or would be in the future, interconnected financially. These discussions were sometimes complicated because of the unease in talking about personal finances, the implications for ongoing relationships, and the possibilities of someone getting hurt.

Multiple financial issues were at work among these elders: some didn't have enough money to be financially independent; some had significant wealth to be distributed to their children and grandchildren; others also had family businesses and property to be passed on. In these matters, some of the elders secured the services of professionals to not only work with the money-management issues but also with family communication and relational questions related to the establishment of new financial responsibilities and the redistribution of funds currently or in a future estate. In each case, direct, accurate, honest communication was crucial to a good outcome.

End-of-Life Planning

Several of the elders had recently updated and discussed with their doctors and families their health and end-of-life directives. In these directives, many were clear about not wanting extraordinary or heroic efforts taken to keep them alive. Some of the elders had also made clear their intentions and expectations regarding assisted living. Some of the elders spoke of having planned their funerals and purchased burial plots. A few of the elders spoke of shedding much of their no longer needed stuff, including offering family keepsakes to family members. Several spoke of updating their wills to reflect theirs and their families' changing situations. Several elders spoke of their comfort in having made these plans as well as of their family's appreciation for what they had done.

> It is equally evident that families can be of great value to their elders.

As I listened to the elders in this study, it is evident that they have the potential for making profound and imaginative contributions to the quality of life of their families. It is equally evident that families can be of great value to their elders. These elders' stories point to the importance of elders and their families reflecting on their interactions and issues and honestly and directly working through them together.

Elders and Their Churches

Faith communities figure significantly in the lives of the elders interviewed. As was described earlier, congregations were major anchoring communities of elder identity, relationships, and support. Most often, the elders were engaged in mutually beneficial relationships with a congregation. They were significant supporters of the ministry of their churches, and the churches were spiritual and social assets for their elders. In two situations, a congregation became both the elders' surrogate family and larger support community.

These elders volunteer in congregations in large numbers. Some lead their congregation's governance and mission by serving on councils and committees as well as initiating and staffing innovative community and international ministries. Some churches reached out to serve elders who were isolated and in financial difficulty. Many congregations visited elders when they were sick and homebound. In so far as they were mobile, the elders faithfully attended worship and contributed. Most of the elders spoke of their congregations as social and spiritual oases.

> The relationship between elders and their congregations clearly holds great promise for enriching elders' lives and strengthening elders' congregations.

The relationship between elders and their congregations clearly holds great promise for enriching elders' lives and strengthening elders' congregations. What follows gathers the experience and wisdom of the fifty-three elders into an expansive missional vision of how a congregation might generatively engage a congregation's elders and the elders in that congregation's surrounding community.

Vital and Resilient Aging Centers

Congregations could enrich elders greatly by exploring, engaging, and embodying the Christian tradition's scriptural and theological understandings of elders and their wisdom in faith and life. They could set out a vision of elders and elderhood emerging and rising. A vision of elderhood might include the affirmations that emerged from exploring Scripture and the Christian traditions, which describe elders as being

- endowed with dignity through birth and baptism;
- responsible for managing the earth in their own time and place;
- called to be storytellers and tradition bearers of God's presence and action;
- conveyors of wisdom and mentors of the young;
- claimed and called by God to serve their neighbors;
- spiritually gifted to equip others and build up the body of Christ, the church;
- gathered, enlightened, and sustained as members of the community of faith; and
- promised abundant eternal life, on their way to a new heaven and earth.

This realistic and robust view of elders and elderhood can inform and inspire a new day of elder identity and of elder presence, purpose, and power in navigating the age wave, enriching older adults' lives, and enhancing societal quality of life.

Combining this theological vision of elders and elderhood with what we've learned regarding wellness and wholeness among elders, congregations can and should become proactively engaged in equipping seniors and their families to develop the assets of elder wellness and wholeness. A major strategic mission of the congregation could be to constructively work with elders on the third chapter of life and its significant shifts—from an elder having been a major family caregiver to becoming a mutual family participant to becoming someone who must rely on family care. Addressing these dynamics is critical to the flourishing of elders and to the strength and health of family relationships. Faith communities can provide information, aid in assessments, and sponsor workshops that enhance elders' physical, mental, emotional, social, financial, ethical, existential, and spiritual functioning. The activities could be led and staffed by elders in the congregation and the community. What's more, the congregations could provide space and host an elder community center or elder gathering place. They could become nodes in a network of senior service providers. Innovative ideas could be crafted and tested in the community via an Elder Corps. Elders could be made available to serve the community through Elders in Action. Congregations could coordinate and facilitate the young and middle elders becoming major supporters and caregivers of the impaired middle and later elders. These congregations could become Centers for Vital and Resilient Aging, advocating for elder issues in the community and promoting a vision of vital aging.

Faith Practices

Most of the elders interviewed are deeply spiritual. Their relationships with God and with others are expressed and strengthened through long-standing faith practices, of which worship and music are primary. Hymns and singing, prayer and liturgy, sermons and study done in the forms they have experienced during a lifetime are the main wellsprings that feed these elders' faith. These elders long for connections to the sacred and are keen to tap their faith as they navigate change, loss, decline, and the narrowing of life into death. Listening to their piety and existential needs and viewing them through the lens of solid theological perspectives, can influence the crafting of worship services, Bible studies, prayer groups, and teaching forums that address the critical spiritual health and life decisions of elders.

Faith Community

Elders often referred to their congregations as "anchoring communities," that is, the people and culture that loved and cared for them and the places where the God narrative and Christian relationships provided identity, belonging, and meaning. Congregations were social centers providing a web of relationships and relational activities that provided friendship and enjoyment. Congregations were a source of healing and support, providing places to recover from hurt and loss. Congregations were pools of new friendships where these elders who had lost those closest to them often found new primary relationships, including new spouses. Congregations were spiritual oases, providing an environment in which the powers of faith, including forgiveness, reconciliation, and hope, were experienced. It is difficult to describe fully or overemphasize the influence faith communities had in the varied contexts of these elders' lives. It is important that faith communities study their own character and dynamics to evaluate how they can enrich the lives of elders in their midst.

Study and Learning

Many of these elders were curious and reflective about their faith, its scope, and its implications for their time in life. They were eager to expand their knowledge of Scripture and their understanding of their beliefs. Many wondered about how to reconcile what they believed with the crises, loss, and chronic and life-threatening illness they or those closest to them were facing. Some had basic life questions they wanted to pursue in the light of their faith. A few doubted and were questioning their faith's veracity and trustworthiness. In addition to faith-related matters, elders wondered about a great many issues related to managing their lives. They wanted more information about health, health care, finances, and family relationships, to name just a few.

> Elders often referred to their congregations as "anchoring communities."

Congregations can be major fountains of learning, tailoring learning opportunities to elders' interests and the challenges they face, perhaps focusing most particularly on the wisdom needed in difficult situations.

Gifts and Strengths

The inevitable transitions in elderhood, such as retirement, slower pace of life, limited mobility, and moving to new living situations, often caused these elders to wonder: "What next?" Many were assisted in this transition by discovering new interests, new passions, new skills, and new callings. Christian faith communities can help elders discover current or potential spiritual gifts that they can exercise for the sake of building up the body of Christ. Congregations can provide tools and processes that elders can use to discover their gifts and then help facilitate the application of the elder's gift(s) within the congregation. Such processes could assist elders in redesigning their lives during times of transition while also enriching the ministry of the whole church. Congregations might add to this spiritual-gifts inquiry an opportunity for elders to review their lives in order to identify the knowledge and skills that have been acquired and developed over the span of their lives. Congregations should take note of elder knowledge and skills and tap them for leadership and service in the church. One might think of faith communities as functioning as spiritual and life-strengths talent scouts and resource pools.

Service

I heard many, many stories of a tremendous variety and volume of volunteering. Most of these elders were robust volunteers; two of them were "super volunteers" and one of them was Volunteer of the Year. Several elders spoke of their congregations as being the creative outlet for their service not only in their congregation but also in their communities and around the world. One congregation organized Grace in Action, a cadre of elders that harnessed the knowledge and skill of the congregation's elders to serve elders in the surrounding area. Many elders were volunteering in schools and for nonprofits. Some were enhancing agriculture, technology, and education internationally. Faith communities can become conduits of elder gifts and talents for serving locally and globally. Congregations could become prime developers of and a locus for an emerging international elder service corps.

Finance

While these elders were at many different places on the socioeconomic spectrum, most of them had both significant discretionary income and accumulated wealth. These elders had greater potential for funding the present and future mission of the church. I envision congregations providing new and innovative ministry resourcing concepts and new stewardship instruments for funding mission. I imagine elders providing mission capital for the outreach opportunities for which they have sensed a call. Elders could help develop a congregation's endowment for the future and thus create a legacy of faith that lives beyond them.

Caregiving

The range of care needed and provided by elders was immense, complicated, exhausting, and inspirational. Elders needed short-term acute care; they needed long-term, progressively more intensive care; they needed assistance with physical limitations following an injury or surgery; they needed accompaniment and therapeutic care following losses; and they required growing attentive supervision as they became more cognitively impaired. Caregivers often needed to be relieved. In this immense and complicated caregiving processes, a huge range of providers—including a great many elders—were engaged in the delicate discernment of what care was needed, as well as how much, where, by whom, and for how long. No matter how these questions were sorted, there often was greater need for care than the caregivers and funding could provide.

While a great many elders, especially those in late elderhood, were being cared for, an extensive number of elders, especially those in early and middle elderhood, were providing care for a spouse, a parent, a sibling, grandchildren, friends, and more. Some elders had cared for parent, spouse, and sibling in succession over long periods of time; a few elders had taken care of more than one person at a time. While this caregiving was crucial, it often took its toll on the caregiver. In some cases, teams of caregivers were needed; in others, *caregiver relievers* helped the primary caregiver to avoid burning out.

While faith communities were tangentially involved in caregiving with these elders, I imagine them having a greater role in the caregiving continuum. A congregation could adopt a parish nursing ministry, which could become an innovative recruiting and coordinating resource in these caregiving challenges. I envision a congregation developing an Elder Caregiving Team of young and middle elders who use their knowledge and skill to participate in certain aspects of caregiving for the older or more frail elders.

I imagine a congregation's Elder Caregiving Team having an exhaustive, categorized list of caregiving options and resources. These Elder Caregiving Teams of young and middle elders would be available to spell spouses and other family members who are providing around-the-clock care for a loved one. A congregation could develop some of its unused space as an Elder Drop-In Center for those with manageable care needs. These centers could be mostly staffed by young and middle elders.

> I imagine a congregation's Elder Caregiving Team having an exhaustive, categorized list of caregiving options and resources.

Intergenerational Innovation and Support

The elders in the study spoke of the power of children in their lives. They valued the relationships they formed with children, young people, and others in congregations. Congregations can provide activities to foster well-springs of quality relationships among the generations, trusting relationships that transmit faith and enrich the quality of life for both the young and elders. Congregations can encourage *companion mentoring*, whereby younger and older persons guide each other in technology usage, life storytelling, vocational discernment, and strengthening faith and enhancing life skills. In a world of often age-segregated daily existence, faith communities are well situated to regularly set the messy tables where dialogue and common action can bring all generations together to promote their common good.

These intergenerational activities and the resulting relationship building can help congregations celebrate elders' lives as well as promote stronger ministry both for elders and for the larger mission of the congregation. Engaging in intergenerational ministry can unlock the developmental assets of elder wellness and wholeness to strengthen elders, their families, the congregation, and society. Some congregations are well on their way to this new day in elder ministry. A sample of these pathfinders is identified at this chapter's end.

Elders Rising and an Elder Corps

Given more extensive investigation and imagination, there may be still more congregations can do. Given the robust Christian understanding of the value of elders and the essential roles they can play, given congregations' powerful communal elder cultures, and given the growing population of elders in their midst, churches are latent resources for enhancing elders rising and incubators for new initiatives to meet the challenges of the age wave. I propose that congregations join others such as Dr. Ken Dychtwald in giving birth to an international Elder Corps.

Many gerontologists speak of developing a national or international organization for harnessing the power of elders to address critical needs in society. They often describe an organization akin to the Peace Corps. One of the best known and most resourceful gerontologists to put forth this idea is Dr. Ken Dychtwald, the founder of Age Wave, an organization studying aging and developing responses to its challenges. Among Dychtwald's proposals is creating "a new purpose for maturity," through mobilizing "a revolutionary global Elder Corps in which tens of millions of boomers are recruited to share their values, knowledge, skills, and wisdom with youth in need."[3] Based on what I learned from the fifty-three elders, there is a large and strong pool of candidates ready for such a mission and organization.

Because the potential for such a mission is reflected in the elders' stories and because elders are so deeply embedded in the life and ministry of their congregations, I propose Christian congregations and faith communities launch experimental Elder Corps, whose mission could include at least some of the following concepts:

- Think Tanks—Investigate and further develop realistic and hope-filled elder identities, lifestyles, and purposes. New models for elders serving could be imagined.

- Dialogue Tables—Gather intergenerational conversation partners to address common issues, such as elder poverty, affordable medical care, childcare, improved K–12 education models, funding lifelong learning, and balanced strategic intergenerational entitlements.

- Information Exchanges—Promote and cultivate expansive elder lifelong learning, ongoing reimagined careers, and flexible, shared work positions/responsibilities.

- Wellness and Wholeness Labs—Promote models of elder wellness and wholeness.

- Age-Specific Service Providers—Address the needs of late elders (age eighty-five plus) as well as the needs of young people.

The Scriptures and theology provide strong, comprehensive understandings of the value of elders and faith communities for pervasive spiritual and social bonds with elders. This means that congregations are well positioned to work together in ecumenical coalitions to launch Elder Corps units in their communities. These experimental Elder Corps units could begin organically and function locally, but as they proliferate and expand, these corps could link up with each other and with other champions of Elder Corps. Together, this loose network with shared purposes and a shared mission can help lead society as it rides the rising age wave.

Exploration and Discussion

1. Eugene Bianchi writes: "Perhaps the most beautiful legacy that aging parents can leave their children is a personally-lived lesson about facing old age and death with courage and grace."[4] Do you agree or disagree with Bianchi? Why? What personal legacy do you want to pass down to others or be remembered for?

2. Imagine re-visioning your faith community by gathering a team of elders to engage your congregation in growing its senior ministry. Consider how you might work on the following:

    - Vital aging center
    - Faith practices
    - Faith community
    - Study and learning
    - Gifts and strengths discovery
    - Service
    - Finance
    - Caregiving
    - Intergenerational innovation and support

3. Ken Dychtwald asserts, "I strongly believe that we should create an organized Elder Corps . . . we need to hear more about what older people can do for young people, for their communities, and for one another."[5] Do you think this is possible? If so, what would it look

like? If an Elder Corps existed, would you consider join-ing? If so, for how long at a time?

4. Two congregations near where I live in Saint Paul, Min-nesota, have launched generative, innovative senior min-istries that embody the notion of Centers for Vital and Resilient Aging:

- Judson Baptist Church in Minneapolis has created "Celebration of Life" videos, which tell the stories and wisdom of elders' lives (see www.judsonchurch .org).

- Redeemer Lutheran Church, White Bear Lake, Minnesota, has created 2nd Half Ministry and also 2nd Half with Lyngblomsten, which is a center for enriching lives of those over fifty (see http://rlc-wbl .org/ministries/seniors/).

Take some time to look at faith communities near you. What, if anything, are they doing to enlist the help of elders in ministry? Do you see any potential partners for creating a local Elder Corps?

Brainstorm what an Elder Corps might look like for your congregation or community.

CONCLUSION

In this investigative foray into older adulthood, I entered through the doorway of my own aging and expanded the inquiry to the lives of fifty-three elders. I put these discoveries into dialog with the Christian tradition and gerontologists' studies on aging and discovered workable insights regarding adults and aging. I discovered folk wisdom, from which several takeaways emerged. Some of the key learnings are as follows:

- Elderhood is a unique, promising stage of life.
- Elderhood is a long, thirty-year stage in the human life cycle.
- Elderhood is a stage of progressive periods that are, to a degree, predictable.
- Elders age in their own unique ways.
- Elderhood is a period of frequent, pervasive, ongoing, impactful change.
- The most disruptive occurrences of elderhood are
  — severe physical disability;
  — debilitating cognitive impairment;

- — isolation; and
- — financial inadequacy.
- ■ Capacities and assets essential to elder resiliency and vitality include
  - — trustworthy relationships;
  - — adaptive management of change;
  - — coping with crisis, especially loss; and
  - — realistic hope.
- ■ Elders have essential societal roles and responsibilities.
- ■ The Scriptures and Christian tradition portray a robust understanding of elders and their essential place in society; this understanding is underdeveloped.
- ■ Faith communities are powerful elder spiritual and social oases; nevertheless, they are underutilized resources for vital and resilient aging.
- ■ Elder resiliency and vitality depend in large part on assessing and nurturing several key dimensions of well-being: physical, mental, emotional, social, financial, ethical, existential, and spiritual.
- ■ Congregations are well situated to give birth to transformational Centers for Vital and Resilient Aging or to provide a base for Elder Corps development.
- ■ If not aggressively and wisely addressed in the next ten years, the advancing age wave will generate an economic and social crisis.

I am deeply grateful for the fifty-three elders who spoke with me about their lives. I have learned much about them, about myself, about elders as a cohort, and about the great promise and substantial risks associated with aging, now and in the future. I look forward to putting these new learnings to work in my own life and in our communities for the larger common good. I look forward to learning more from your own ongoing investigation and discussion regarding the powerfully advancing wave of elders and their influence on our culture. I'm excited and eager to be an active participant in elders rising!

NOTES

CHAPTER 1: THE AGE WAVE AND EARLY NAVIGATORS

1. Ken Dychtwald, "How the Age Wave Will Transform the Marketplace, the Workplace and Our Lives," Age Wave, https://tinyurl.com/ybowca4m.
2. "A New Vision for 21st Century Aging: Five Course Corrections Needed for a Century of Healthy, Active and Successful Aging," American Society on Aging, https://tinyurl.com/y7pcl5q3.
3. See John W. Rowe and Robert L. Kahn, *Successful Aging* (New York: Pantheon, 1998), and Paul Taylor, *Growing Old in America: Expectations vs Reality* (Washington, DC: Pew Research Center, 2009).

CHAPTER 2: AGING AND THE CHRISTIAN FAITH

1. Paul Taylor, *Growing Old in America: Expectations vs Reality* (Washington, DC: Pew Research Center, 2009).
2. See Joyce Ann Mercer, "Older Adulthood: Vocation at Life's End," in *Calling All Years Good: Christian Vocation Throughout Life's Seasons*, ed. Kathleen A. Cahalan and Bonnie J. Miller-McLemore (Grand Rapids: Eerdmans, 2014), 178.

3. Justin Gammill, "The 4 Stages of Life according to Carl Jung," IHeartIntelligence.com, October, 28, 2015, https://tinyurl.com /ybzn7w9f.

CHAPTER 3: ELDERHOOD: A NEW LIFE STAGE

1. "A New Vision for 21st Century Aging: Five Course Corrections Needed for a Century of Healthy, Active and Successful Aging," American Society on Aging, https://tinyurl.com/y7pcl5q3.
2. Justine Willis Toms and Mary Catherine Bateson, "Adulthood II: A Whole New Stage in the Life Cycle," *New Dimensions*, ABC, March 14, 2011, https://tinyurl.com/y8hd2r5r. See also Mary Catherine Bateson, *Composing a Further Life: The Age of Active Wisdom* (New York: Knopf, 2010).
3. Paul Taylor, *Growing Old in America: Expectations vs Reality* (Washington, DC: Pew Research Center, 2009).
4. Laura L. Carstensen, "In Search of a Word That Won't Offend 'Old' People," *Washington Post*, December 29, 2017, https:// tinyurl.com/yajcyz8v.
5. See G. Oscar Anderson, "2016 Technology Trends among Mid-Life and Older Americans," AARP Research, November 2016, https://tinyurl.com/yd357uoh.
6. See John W. Rowe and Robert L. Kahn, *Successful Aging* (New York: Pantheon, 1998). Rowe and Kahn are members of the MacArthur Foundation Research Foundation on Successful Aging.

CHAPTER 4: PRESENCE: THE CAPACITY TO ACCOMPANY

1. Brigid Schulte, *Overwhelmed: Work, Love, and Play When No One Has the Time* (New York: Sarah Crichton Books, 2014).

CHAPTER 5: RELATIONSHIPS: BETTER TOGETHER

1. Chris Farrell, "The Painful Struggles of America's Older Immigrants," *Next Avenue*, TPT/PBS, December 9, 2016, https://

tinyurl.com/ydaxbc2j; on Paul Tang's work, see Sheila Zinck, "Combating Loneliness in the Aging Population," IBM, May 10, 2017, https://tinyurl.com/y8aqwtl5.

CHAPTER 7: PURPOSE: MAKING A DIFFERENCE

1. See "Having a Purpose in Life May Improve Health of Aging Brain," American Heart Association, March 19, 2015, https://tinyurl.com/ychq7yem.

CHAPTER 9: PLAYFULNESS: ENJOYMENT AND LEISURE

1. See Careen Yarnal and Xinyi Qian, "Older-Adult Playfulness: An Innovative Construct and Measurement for Healthy Aging Research," *American Journal of Play* 4, no. 1 (Summer 2011): 52–79.

CHAPTER 10: PERIL: VULNERABILITY AND RESILIENCY

1. MacArthur Foundation Research Network on an Aging Society, "Facts and Fictions about an Aging Society," *Contexts* 8, no. 4 (2009): 16–21.

CHAPTER 11: LIVING WITH LOSS

1. Mohsin Hamid, Sydney Writers Festival, Sydney, Australia, May 2015.
2. This quote has been commonly attributed to Washington Irving since at least *The Young Ladies' Journal* (E. Harrison, 1868), 156.
3. See Elisabeth Kübler-Ross and David Kessler, *On Grief and Grieving: Finding the Gift of Grief through the Five Stages of Mourning* (New York: Simon & Schuster, 2005). See also "7 Stages of Grief: Through the Process and Back to Life," Recover-from-Grief.com, https://tinyurl.com/ybuerttn.
4. Permission to reprint the poem has been granted by the writer.

CHAPTER 12: NAVIGATING CHANGE

1. This prayer has become known as "The Holden Prayer" and is often referred to as the "Lutheran Prayer of Good Courage."

CHAPTER 13: ELDERS RISING

1. Matt Dabbs, "Rabbi Abraham Heschel on Old Age and Facing Death," *Kingdom Living* (blog), January 12, 2009, https://tinyurl .com/ydydrd8o.
2. Bob Ramsey, "Seniors Can Create a 'Mosaic of Activities,'" *Sun Current*, September 15, 2016, p. 5, https://tinyurl.com/yap94748.
3. See "Active Aging and Wellness: Seven Dimensions of Wellness," International Council on Active Aging, https://tinyurl.com /y759rnk8.

CHAPTER 14: ELDERS RISING: FAMILIES AND CHURCHES

1. Ken Dychtwald, *Age Power: How the 21st Century Will Be Ruled by the New Old* (New York: Putnam, 2000), 266.
2. Eugene C. Bianchi, *Aging as a Spiritual Journey* (New York: Crossroad, 1984), 169.
3. Ken Dychtwald, "Do Boomers Have the Guts and Wisdom to Course Correct Our Aging Nation," *Huffington Post*, May 11, 2013, https://tinyurl.com/ycu83top.
4. Bianchi, *Aging as a Spiritual Journey*, 169.
5. Dychtwald, *Age Power*, 266.

THEOLOGY FOR CHRISTIAN MINISTRY

Informing and inspiring Christian leaders and communities to proclaim God's *Word* to a *World* God created and loves. Articulating the fullness of both realities and the creative intersection between them.

Word & World Books is a partnership between Luther Seminary, the board of the periodical *Word & World*, and Fortress Press. Other books in the series include the following:

Future Faith: Ten Challenges Reshaping Christianity in the 21st Century by Wesley Granberg Michaelson (978-1-5064-3344-8)

Liberating Youth from Adolescence by Jeremy Paul Myers (978-1-5064-3343-1)